CARVING

THE

HUMAN

FACE

Capturing Character and
Expression in Wood

by Jeff Phares

Publisher: Alan Giagnocavo
Project Editor: Ayleen Stellhorn
Desktop Specialist: Linda L. Eberly, Eberly Designs Inc.
Interior Photography: Marc Featherly
Cover Photography: Marc Featherly

ISBN # 1-56523-102-3

To order your copy of this book,
please send check or money order
for $24.95 plus $2.50 shipping to:
Fox Books Orders
1970 Broad Street
East Petersburg, PA 17520

Printed in Hong Kong

Acknowledgements

This book is in memory of my Grandfather Kyle Phares. He always had faith and believed in me and what I was doing. I would like to offer my gratitude to my family and friends for their continued support and patience, and my thanks to photographer Marc Featherly for the outstanding photography within these pages. You are the best. My thanks also go to the Carvers that have had a hand in helping and motivating me to do what I love best, carving. I would also like to thank you guys, and you know who you are, for your constant encouragement to be the best that I can be. Last but not least, a very warm special thanks to LMG–BO and the staff at Casa Nogata for all the last minute details.

· TABLE OF CONTENTS ·

Working with the Blank
…page 9

Establishing the Face
…page 11

Outlining the Scarf
…page 19

Roughing in the Headdress
…page 26

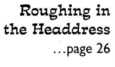

Creating the Hair Wraps
…page 30

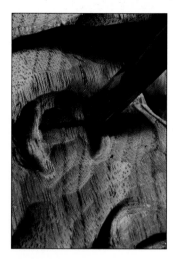
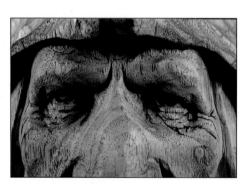

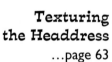

• TABLE OF CONTENTS •

Varnishing the Carving
...page 76

Applying Wax
...page 80

Painting the Mask
...page 77

Hair Wraps
...page 83

Knots
...page 85

Eyes
...page 87

Nose
...page 88

Foreword

When I first decided to write this book, *Carving the Human Face,* I was eager to share my knowledge of wood carving with my fellow enthusiast. Throughout the writing and completion of this book, I found myself continually inspired as I hope you the reader will be as well.

I have provided you with a step-by-step, instructional guide to produce the project supplied within these pages. Upon completion of this book, you will have a finished project to enjoy, as well as have learned new techniques and methods that will be valuable to your personal wood carving projects in the future.

I sincerely hope that you will enjoy working with my book as much as I have enjoyed putting it together.

Good carving,
Jeff Phares

On Design

Coming up with an idea or a subject is the first part of the carving process. However, as far as explaining, teaching or trying to tell someone else how to do that is easier said than done.

Nevertheless, here are a few things to think about before you begin a carving.

First: What would I like to look at? What subject do I want to use? What interests me? For the subject for this book, I choose a Native American wearing a wolf headdress.

Second: Find research material. Look for photos or models or other artwork. Get as close to your subject as you can. For my subject, I started with photos of Indian faces. I familiarized myself with the different characteristics of faces: noses, cheekbones, eyes, anatomy profiles, side views...Then I found reference material on the "accessories," in this case, the wolf headdress. I looked for drawings and photographs of a wolf skin, as well as a skin itself. I used all the reference material I could find to create a mental picture of my subject.

Third: Decide on making a bust or a mask. A bust is the head and shoulders of a subject carved in the round. A mask is a hollowed out version of the subject's face. I chose to carve a mask.

Fourth: Sketch your idea using some basic design rules to create good line, flow and continuity. Work with S-curves, C-curves, circles and triangles. In the Diagram section of this book, you'll see some of the sketches I made before I began to carve this piece. Bear in mind, "the pencil" and I do not get along that well. I would be the last person to tell someone I could draw,

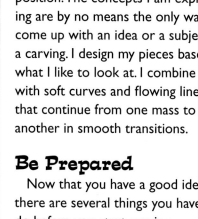

This is one of the photographs we chose not to use in the demonstration section of this book. The photographer, Marc Featherly, and I took three very long days to shoot all the photos for the demonstration section of this book.

but my sketches are good enough for me to see what I am planning to carve. I consider myself living proof that you don't have to be able to draw well to carve.

A whole book could be written on design and composition. The concepts I am explaining are by no means the only way to come up with an idea or a subject for a carving. I design my pieces based on what I like to look at. I combine that with soft curves and flowing lines that continue from one mass to another in smooth transitions.

Be Prepared

Now that you have a good idea, there are several things you have to do before you start carving. Drawing a pattern is first on the agenda. For a mask I draw a front view and a profile. (See the pattern on page 104.)

Next is choosing your wood. Basswood is probably the best wood to start your carving. I have had experience carving many different woods, including walnut, red cedar, juniper, butternut and basswood. I prefer to use butternut or basswood. Butternut is the wood I chose to use for the demonstration in this book.

Last, but not least is assembling the tools you'll need. I'm including a list of the tools I used

I use a wide variety of tools in this demonstration. Shown here are a number of the tools in my workshop.

while carving the piece in this book. You do not need all of these tools to carve this piece. I have been carving — and collecting — tools for a number of years. I have my favorites, which I use repeatedly. I also have many other tools that I rarely use. The key is to use the tools that you are familiar with and that will give you the same results as the results in the demonstration. I've starred the tools that I believe are essential.

*knife
#1, 2 mm skew (eye clean up)
*#3, 1 mm (shaping the face)
#3, 14 mm
#5, 30 mm (removing waste)
*#5, 16 mm (face work)
#7, 25 mm
#7, 14 mm
*#7, 10 mm (nose)
*#8, 18 mm long bent (block out)
#8, 8 mm
#8, 3 mm (pupil)
#9, 20 mm
#9, 13 mm
*#9, 10 mm
#11, 15 mm
*#11, 10 mm
*#11, 5 mm (eyes)
#11, 3 (nostril)

V-tools
*#13, 10 mm (lips)
#12, 8 mm
#14, 10 mm

Specialty Tools
#11, 5 mm spoon
#28, 10 mm back bent

About Sharpening

As with any aspect of carving, I could go on and on... but for the purposes of this book, simple and effective are the two points to keep in mind when thinking about sharpening your tools. Regardless of the wood you're using or the subject you're carving, *sharp tools are a necessity.* As with anything, it is best to learn from the ground up. Learn to use a stone and a hand strop before you move on to other methods of sharpening your tools.

Getting Started

When you've obtained your wood and have your tools out and sharp, you're ready to begin carving. Apply the pattern to the block, either by tracing it or using carbon paper as a transfer. The block of wood I'm using for this demonstration is 4 inches thick by 8 inches wide by 14 inches tall. I have bandsawed the front view according to the pattern. We will be creating the profile from scratch. Take a look at the pieces in the gallery, then let's get started on one of your own.

Shown here is a typical carver's arm and screw set up. I use this on virtually everything. The arms can be purchased or built to suit your needs. The screws are best purchased from your favorite supply shop.

Don
Hand Ramsey Ranch, KS
bust
butternut
14" tall

Campos Cookfire
bust
catalpa, natural with dark
wax finish
22" tall

Untitled Cowboy bust,
catalpa, natural finish
20" tall

Eli
bust
basswood
10" tall

Clemons
cottonwood bark
10" tall

Untitled
bust
juniper, natural finish
14" tall

Study faces
basswood
3" x 5" x 7"

Stands His Ground
bust, basswood
18" tall

Two Bears
mask
butternut
7" x 16" x 18"

Untitled
Mountain man mask
basswood
4" x 8" x 14

GALLERY

Untitled
Native American study
Butternut, 15" tall

Untitled Indian Mask
Basswood/natural
4" x 7" x 13"

Untitled
red cedar
22" tall

Father Christmas
basswood
12" tall

Untitled
butternut
7" x 16" x 18"

Crooked Crow
basswood, stained from solid block
9" x 12" x 18"

Gives His Horse
wormy butternut
16" tall, 18" with base

Portrait of Grandfather,
E. Kyle Phares
bust
clay

Untitled
French trapper mask,
basswood
4" x 8" x 14"

GALLERY

Untitled
Mountain man bust
butternut, monochrome finish, 16" tall

Untitled Large Relief Carving
(eagle at one inch thick, up to eight inches thick
at the horse's hoof)
basswood, natural finish
Collection of the artist

Untitled
mask, butternut
approx. 14" tall

The author carves this mask in
the following demonstration.

1 With the bandsaw, I cut out the front view of the pattern. (See the pattern in the Diagram section.) I mark the centerline, then I mark lines 1 inch from the centerline on both sides of the centerline.

2 I turn the block to the side, or "edge," and mark a line 1 1/2 inches in from the back of the block running the length of the piece.

3 On the bottom of the block, I mark a centerline. I drill a 1/4 inch hole about 1 inch in from the back of the block and about 1–2 inches deep. I crank the screw in as tightly as I possibly can. I have yet to split a block in half.

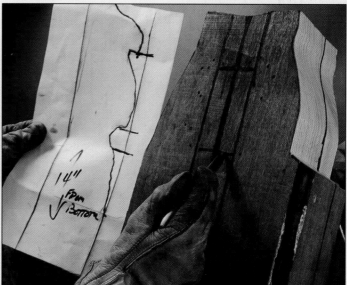

4 Just a few more markings and I can start carving. Here I am holding up a profile of the piece. Note the three marks I've made on the profile: the bottom of the headdress, the chin of the Indian head, and about where the scarf would start. These three markings give me some general guidelines. When you are working on your piece, you may choose to bandsaw the profile. I am working from a rough front view, so I am going to block the profile out from scratch. I always allow a little extra room at the top and a little extra room for the back.

5 I start with a #5, 3-inch-wide fishtail-style gouge, working the block into a wedge shape. Notice that I am working from the marks on each side of the centerline out to the line I made at the edge. These guidelines give me plenty of wood to the side and plenty of width in the center of the face.

6 I work both sides of the block. The fishtail-style gouge quickly removes large pieces of wood.

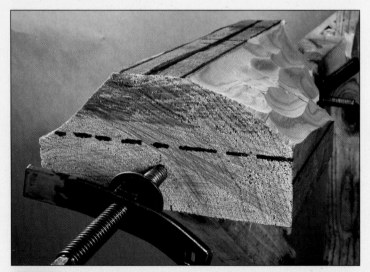

7 Here you can see both sides of the blank are "wedged back," and there is a flat spot down the center. Notice how the cuts relate to the guidelines I marked on the wood. These first cuts are beginning to give some shape to the piece.

8 I am still using the wide #5 gouge. Notice the marks on the front of the piece where the wolf head, the chin, and the top of the scarf were marked in.

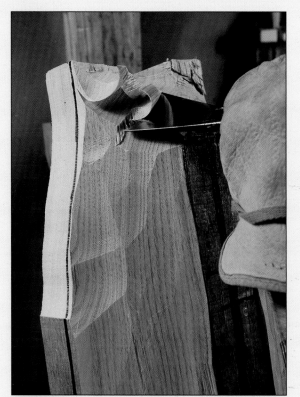

9 I give the wolf headdress a wedge shape and a kind of triangular shape. You can see how I am working back to the line I made on the edge of the piece.

10 Here you can see how I have come underneath and across the front to establish the bottom of the wolf's nose. I have roughed in the bottom of the chin and removed some wood across the center of the chest. Now I am using a large #9 gouge to start the line around the headdress and around face of the Indian.

11 See how the line on the left side of the face has been established? That is the beginning of the Indian's head, the hair and the face. Notice the dark spots on the wood. Those are the uncut surfaces of the block; I am leaving myself plenty of width. Notice the headdress line has been drawn in on the right side of the face, just generally.

12 This photograph shows the face from a different angle. The headdress and the chin are established. I am now working up the right side of the face, removing some wood to establish the sides of the facial mass, and to separate the head from the headdress a little better.

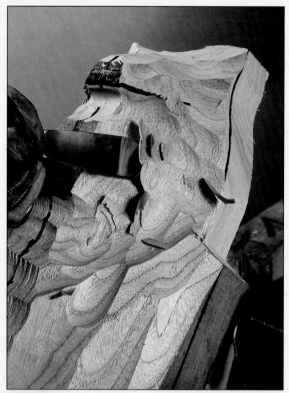

13 Here I am using a #2 gouge. This tool is almost a flat chisel. I am working back, establishing a sharper line and giving the face a little more of a wedge shape. I am pulling in the edges of the face so the face can be surrounded by the headdress.

14 This profile view shows the beginnings of the face and the headdress. The line that you see drawn in this picture marks the hair line.

15 This is the opposite side of the piece. See the relationship to the line I drew down the edge of the block in the beginning? These reference points serve as great reminders and keep me from removing too much wood too quickly.

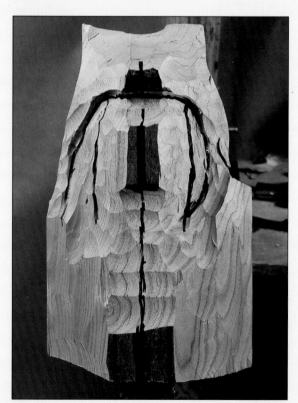

16 On this front view of the carving, you can still see the dark spots where I haven't carved away the surface of the block yet. I try to think in shapes, forgetting any detail whatsoever at this point. I have drawn in the area where the hair is going to be and the line where the headdress is coming down. I have also started removing some wood on the top to create some shape to the top of the head. All this is still general shaping.

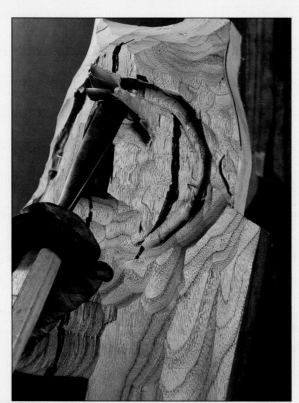

17 Here I am using a wide #2 gouge (a #3 will also work) to slope the forehead back up underneath the headdress, basically from the point of the nose back. I want to create a good profile. I have also taken wood off the front of the wolf's nose and redrawn a centerline on the front of the nose.

18 I shape the line around the head with a #3 fishtail gouge. This is a stopcut. This is an important line because everything is built around its position. Notice that the wolf head looks pretty tall on the top of the head. That is fine. I can always take it down later.

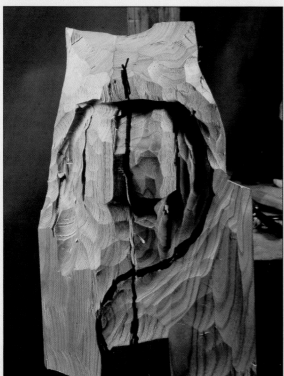

19 On this photograph, notice the centerline. I stopped carving halfway. The hair line and the face are blocked out. The big "S" curve that you see drawn in here is where the edge of the cape is going to lie. Notice it covers one side of the carving; the other side will be left open. Now I need to concentrate on getting the other side of the face shaped down to match the side I've been working on.

20 A profile view of the piece shows how much wood was removed to create the basic shapes of the carving: the chest, face and neck, hair, cape and wolf headdress.

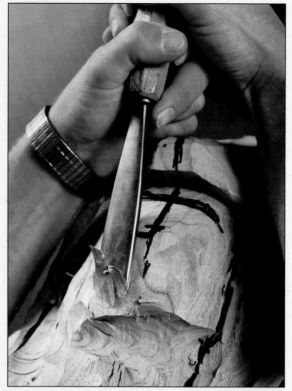

21 Continuing on, I am still using the wide #2 gouge. It is almost flat, but not quite. This makes it a good shaping tool. Here I am cutting down from the point of the nose to pull back the chin. These cuts will strengthen and shape the profile a little better.

22 You can see the general shape that I have created. I am coming underneath the chin and around the neck area, pushing the jaw line back to the hair line that I drew in. This will create the angle of the jaw. (A good rule of thumb to remember is that the angle of the jaw is either at 4 o'clock or 8 o'clock, depending which side of the head you are working on.)

23 Here is a side view of the carving so far. Notice the line that I drew down the edge of the block in the beginning is still present. This is an important line. I have left the wood behind it untouched. Following that line ensures that I will have enough wood in the back of the piece.

24 Take a close look at the profile of the face. The line indicates the top of the skull. You can see the masses beginning to take shape. Notice the shape of the wolf head as it slopes up to the top of the block. Also notice how the nose hangs down in the eyes of the Indian.

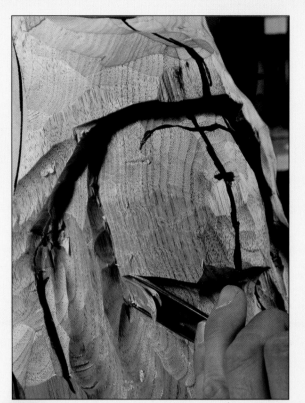

25 Here is a front view of the work I have just completed. You can see that the hair masses are separated. The face, the headdress and the hair are clearly blocked in.

26 Now I work the neck back a little more to create a stronger angle to the jaw. I am using a #9 gouge, about 3/4 inch wide. A tip: Always try to use the biggest tool you can get your hands on that will fit the spot on which you are working. In this photograph you can also see the line for the brow ridge and the bottom of the nose. Those positions may change as I go along, but they are just guidelines to help me to keep everything in perspective and proportion as I carve.

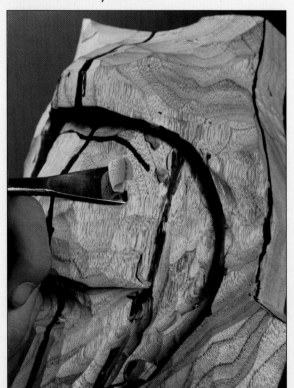

27 Did you notice that the centerline is always present? That line is very important. When I cut the centerline off, I always put it back on right away. It helps me to keep things symmetrical. Here I am working back from the point of the nose along the cheek with a #3 fishtail gouge, about 1 inch wide. This area needs to be swept back along the side of the nose, still leaving a slightly flat center spot up the center of the nose.

28 I establish the face shape where the hairline meets the face. That will give me the final face shape. I am working with a #3 gouge. I push the tool in along the temple and create a slightly hollow area. I stop cut into where the temple meets the hair.

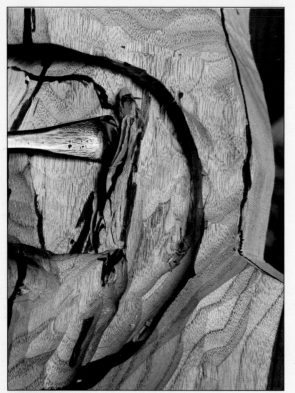

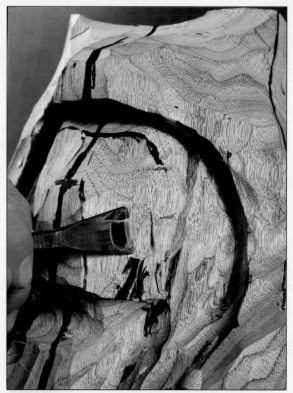

29 Now I am taking the #3 gouge and flipping it over. I am using the rounding aspect of it to shape the cheekbones or, in anatomical terms, the zygomatic arch. This will give the cheekbones a rounded shape all the way back to where the hair meets the face.

30 Flipping the gouge over again, I am creating a hollowed-out area underneath the cheek bone. This is the area where the side of the face will slope down to the jaw.

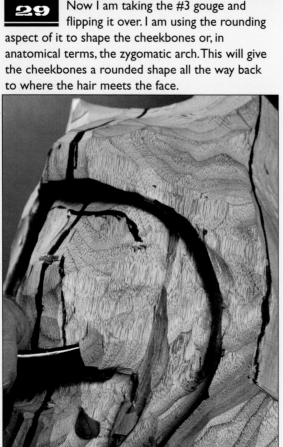

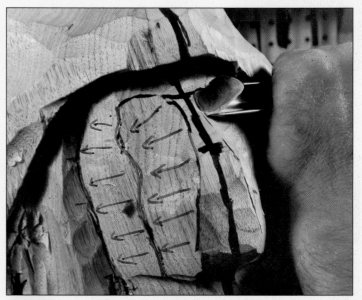

31 Here I am using the gouge upside down again to round the jaw bone back to where the hair meets the face. Creating this line down the side of the face gives me a nice shape and separates the hair from the face.

32 In this photograph, you can see the three planes of the face: the front, the corner and the side. The arrows in the photo show the directions I work the gouge to establish the planes. I am starting to establish the eye socket and create the brow ridge. A tip: Make sure you have the planes established before you start working on the brow ridge and scooping out the eye sockets.

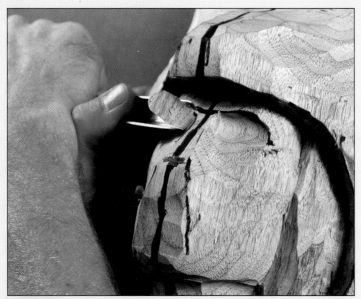

33 Here you can see the left side of the face is done and I am now working on the right side of the face. I am using a #9, 13 gouge to start establishing the secondary profile (the corner of the face). I am also creating a brow ridge. Notice how close the brow ridge is drawn to the headdress. This is the trick to doing a piece with a hat: The hat or headdress should be pulled down close to the eye so there's not a lot of forehead. That gives the hat a natural, relaxed, realistic fit when the brow ridge is drawn.

34 I use a #9 gouge to further establish the eye sockets. You can start to see the mouth area and the end of the nose coming out.

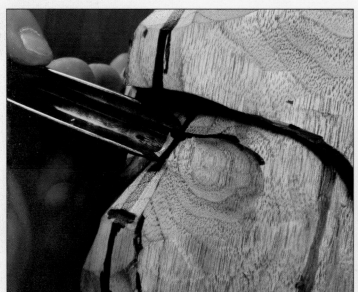

35 Notice here the flat spot across the bridge of the nose and down the center of the face. This allows me plenty of width so I don't get the nose too sharp. Here I have a #11 gouge and I am establishing the bridge of the nose. Notice the brow line, the shape of the face, and the protruding mouth area. Those are three features that create a good, strong face. You must have a good shape to begin with for all the details to look right.

36 I use a #3 again to create a smooth transition of form. In this case, that means a smooth change from one shape to another. I am working on the transitions from the nose to the cheekbone. The area under the eye and down around the side of the mouth area has to be swept away and carved back at an angle. Remember to create a smooth transition from here to the cheekbone and nose as well.

37 I use the #3 again to shape the mouth area. I taper the chin in toward the center of the mouth area to make the chin narrow. The widest point of the face is the cheek bone. The second widest is the forehead. The third widest is the jaw and chin area.

38 Here I have a #7, 14 mm gouge and I am rounding over the top of the nose, and right up to the bridge. As you can see in the photograph, there is a small, thin cut-line between the eyes. That is where I am rounding to. I use the gouge upside down to get the roundness. A #7 and a #5 are the tools to use to get good shapes for noses.

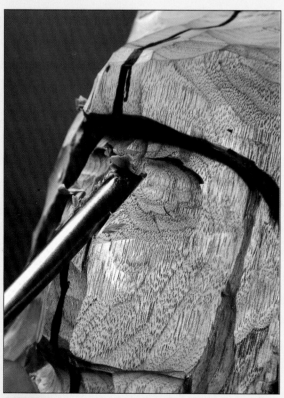

39 Using the same #7, I am going up the side of the nose and cleaning up a little better in to the corner area of the eyes.

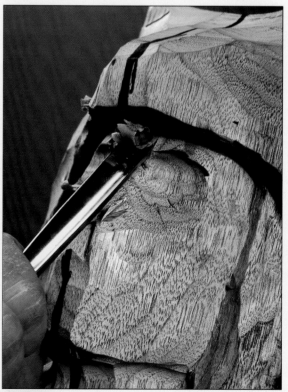

40 I turn the gouge right side up, working between the eyebrows and up to the center of the headdress. This creates a slight indentation between the eyebrow ridges.

41 In this photo, notice the shape of the face, the brow and the bridge of the nose. The headdress line and the hair masses are established. Everything appears a little wide, but as I carve, everything will gradually narrow in. Also notice that I have drawn some lines to finish out my design. I use slow flowing curves. The cross-hatched areas will be cut out. The scarf and the hair are drawn in to give me a general idea of this piece. Now it's just a matter of blocking the rest of the piece out.

42 I use the #11 gouge again (or a #9 will work) to outline the hair ties and the scarf. The neck has to appear to recede, so I need to bring the scarf out. There are three levels to this scarf: the round, center slide; the scarf itself; and then the neck.

43 I continue to work on the same area. Here you see the cut that was created in the previous photo (42).

44 I use a #9 to work out the area underneath the scarf.

45 I have the center slide outlined. I have the neck pushed back and part of the chest area hole dug. Now I am starting to shape the ties that hang off the bottom of the scarf. Notice the different levels on which I am working.

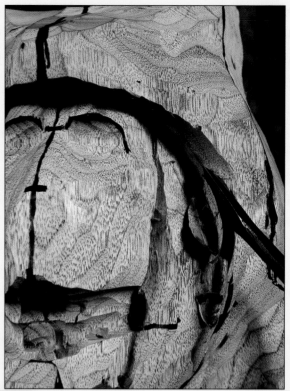

46 I use a #3 gouge to clean up the face shape and the side of the hair. This is how I finalize the hat line. Carve the hair in to fit the hat. The angle of the tool is what keeps the cut good and clean. I will create somewhat of an undercut, but I'm not cutting very deep. I want clean sharp lines, not a deep undercut.

47 Time for a break. Here is a picture of the shop. The particular holding device I am using is a basic three-section carving arm and a "Burke Woodcarving Screw." Well, my photographer Marc is giving me the look so it's back to work.

48 In this photograph, you can see a good shot of the face shape, the hair masses and the scarf and slide. I have a #7, 1/2 inch gouge and I am tucking the neck down into the top of the scarf. This is another example of smooth transition of form: A smooth change from the chin and the jaw to the neck.

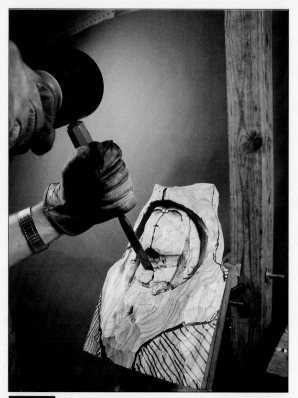

49 Here is a larger view of the whole scene. I have a #4 gouge, 10–14 mm wide. I am establishing a sharp cut, straight in, to give the top of the slide the shape it needs. I put the gouge in upside-down and use the shape of the gouge to create the roundness of the slide.

50 The slide is the first thing I have to work on because it is farthest out on the scarf and neck area. See the outlined cuts around it? I am using a #3 gouge upside-down to round over or create a positive shape to the slide.

51 I remove some wood from around the slide, bringing the slide decoration out even more.

52 I make cuts that will tuck the neck down in behind the scarf.

53 I use the #7 gouge upside-down to round off the top side of the scarf area and wrap it right around the neck. There are three areas that meet in this corner: the neck, the scarf, and the hair. The hair is on the outside of everything; the scarf is next; the neck is inside the scarf. I keep their respective levels in mind while I carve.

54 I start to shape the robe and the cape with a #5, 30 mm gouge. I constantly work back toward the shoulders. The cross-hatched areas will be removed. I have begun carving the basic neck shape. I treat the neck area like a tube in the center and everything tapers back from that.

55 Here is the other side. You can start to see how the chest and the hair start to shape up at this stage of the game. The headdress looks pretty big and bulky, so it is time to shape it down to fit everything else I have so far. Here I am using a #5 again, shaping the headdress to fit the head.

56 I use the large #7 gouge again to shape the robe and the cape. I am working on making the wolf skin fit the piece and removing any squareness. I create some shape by working from the front toward the outside edge. I am doing just general shaping at this point.

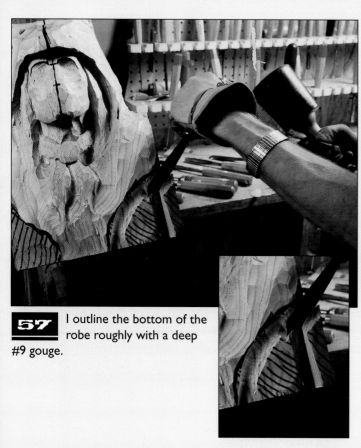

57 I outline the bottom of the robe roughly with a deep #9 gouge.

58 With a large #5, I take off big chunks to get the waste out of the way. These cuts will help to get rid of some of the squareness and give some shape to the piece.

59 Another view shows how the wood comes off.

60 I use a #9 (or #11) gouge again to outline the bottom of the robe on the other side.

61 I want the robe to appear to be underneath the scarf ties, so now I have to shape the scarf ties down a little bit more so they will lie flatter on the chest. I make sure everything fits as I go, working all over the carving.

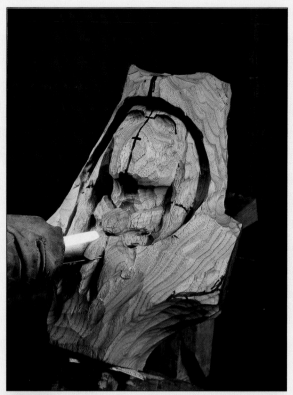

62 Again, I am working on the scarf ties and getting them shaped down and everything else pushed back. I don't want the ties to stick out farther than the chin.

63 Notice the shape of the face, the hair masses, the definite line where the headdress meets the head, how the scarf is blocked out, and the shape of the neck. You can now see generally how this thing is going to look. (Proportion guidelines: The bottom of the nose is the halfway mark between the bridge of the nose and the chin.)

64 Here is a close-up shot of the face at a three-quarter angle view. I marked the bottom of the nose, the top of the wrappings for the hair, and the brow line.

65 The same shot from the front.

66 This photo shows an overall side view. I want you to notice the profile and the depth. Notice the depth of the robe in this photo. That will come back a lot more. That helps bring the face and the hair more out toward the front.

67 Notice the shapes in this close-up view. If there are any adjustments that need to be made, now is the time to make them.

68 Notice how the scarf is back behind the chin. Notice the smooth transition from the chin to the neck and how the neck goes into the shoulders at an angle back.

69 Here is an overall front view. I have the centerlines marked. My next step for blocking out this piece is getting the hat shaped to the head. You can see the markings I plan to follow. I have marked where the eye brow ridge of the animal and the front edge of the ears.

70 I have labeled the planes on the headdress. Section A is from the nose back o the eye brows. Section B is from the brows to the front of the ears. Section C is the ears.

71 I use a large #7 gouge to rough out the headdress. I have to shape the wolf skin to make it look like it fits on top of the Indian's head. I start removing some wood to establish the fronts of the ears. I am carving right in front of the ears (Section B).

72 Again, I use the #7 gouge to carve out in front of the wolf's eye. On the wolf's left side, you can see the results of the cuts I made. I make cuts in front of the brow line that you see and in front of the eye brow to establish the brow.

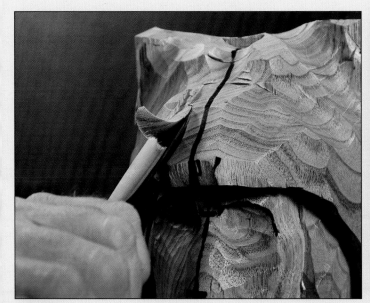

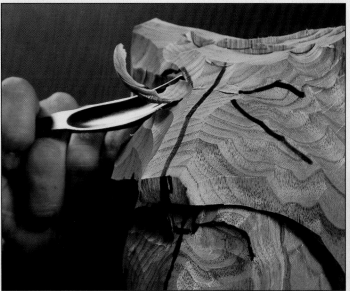

73 On the left side you can see the brow is now established. The plane of the nose on the wolf head has been defined a little bit. Notice here I have a flat spot down the center of the nose. This guarantees I will have plenty of wood to finish the headdress.

74 Here I am using a large #8, 18 mm to cut out at the socket area. On the left side I have drawn in the eye socket area. Remember this is a dried skin, not a live animal; everything is a little different.

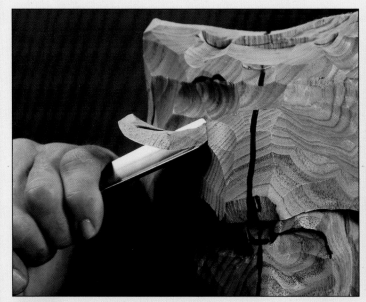

75 Now that I have the socket area formed I work on the nose underneath the socket. You can see the wolf head beginning to take shape. I still have a lot of height and a lot of wood left up on top, but I can always take that down later.

76 You can see the eye socket defined a little bit more, and I have also brought the top of the forehead down. You can see where I stopped cutting. I start to shape in the ear a little better and clean off the top of the block.

77 I use a #7 gouge (a #5 or any type of gouge like that will also work) and clean off the back edge of the block. This will prevent the back from splitting off as I shape the top of the headdress.

78 Here I am working on the top of the wolf's head. I have the brow and the nose shaped in. I always work all over the piece to progress it at the same rate.

79 I use a wide #5 gouge to carve up over the ear, slightly rounding it forward.

80 Most of the preliminary shaping has been done. On the headdress, you can see a definite definition between the brow ridge and the nose and the ears. I have drawn in the ears. One ear will be sticking up and one will be curled over. Adding some irregularity gives everything a much more natural appearance, which is something to keep in mind when you are designing your piece. I have the eyes and the nostrils marked. With all this laid out, I am now ready to carve the piece down.

82 On this close-up view, notice how I made the head-dress fit the head. The brow of the animal is just about where the top of the Indian's head would be. This placement makes everything look like it fits naturally.

81 Notice how everything is sloping back. Thinking in those terms will keep all your carvings from being too flat, which is a common mistake for all of us. Also note that I have shaped the wolf head. Though you can't see it in this photo, I have curled the left ear over so it's pointing down. That gives the piece a little bit of relaxation and more of a natural look.

84 OK. I have the wolf cap shaped down to fit the head. I have a good shape for the face. I have the hair masses blocked out, and the basic outline of the piece is there. Now I just need to refine everything. I am going to start with the scarf ties because they are basically on the outside of everything. Here I am using a #3 fishtail gouge. I make a stop cut, using the shape of the gouge to shape the tie.

83 Here is an overall side view. I check the profile. I check the shape of everything. Notice how the chest and scarf are back behind the chin. If any adjustments need to be made, I make them now.

85 I remove wood from around the ties, actually cutting away the cape around it to bring the ties up. You can see how I am using the gouge to create the shapes for the scarf ends that hang down.

86 I use a #9 gouge to outline the ends of the hair wraps. I do this on both sides and clean up any areas around them that need to be cleaned. As you'll notice, I have quite a pile of chips hanging around; it is time to take them off.

87 I now have the ties blocked out. You can see that the tie on the right side is pretty much shaped and separated. Here I am using a #3 gouge to taper the hair down into the top of the wrap.

88 I use a V-tool to outline the top of the wrap.

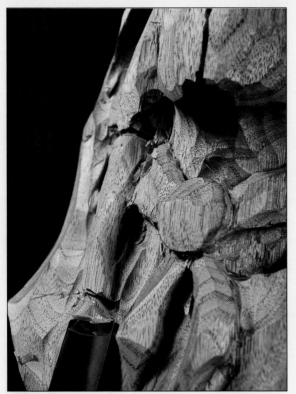

89 Using a flat #7 (or #5) gouge, I take the tassel of the hair that hangs below the wrap and tuck it up into the bottom of the wrap.

90 I cut the hair wrap out with a #7 gouge and create some twists in it all at the same time. The trick to doing a hair tie or a hair wrap is when you are initially shaping it out. You define the top and bottom and then carve the wrapped section down, to "shrink" it, so to speak. Leave the hair on both ends. That tends to make it look tight.

92 I am now working on the wolf cape. I use a #3 gouge to establish the top line that comes down across the Indian's chest.

91 Here you can see everything is pretty well blocked out. The wolf headdress is shaped; one ear is shaped and the other ear is drawn in. You can see where I have stopped and drawn some lines for reference points. Notice the outline of the wolf headdress, how it flows around the piece. Notice the shapes of the hair wraps and the scarf. Here I am just removing some wood in the negative area that is going to be cut out later.

93 To carve out the chest I use a #9 gouge. This wood doesn't have to be there, so at this point, I usually just dig it back as far as I can to get it out of the way. Then I can work on the rest of the piece more easily.

94 Here is an overall front view of everything up to this point. Notice how all the components of the carving are established (except of the little piece of hair that hangs below the robe on the Indian's left side). Notice the curving line that establishes the bottom edge of the wolf skin. This is how you want to shape your piece. Everything I have cross-hatched will be gone on the final piece.

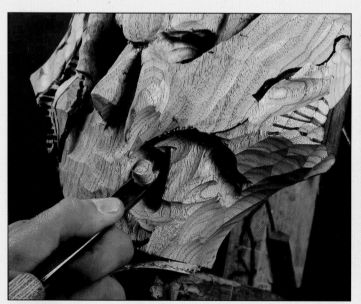

95 Now I am going to work on this little piece of hair. I want to make it look like it is an extension of the hair braid that comes down underneath the robe and cut away wood around that piece of hair.

96 I use a wide gouge to establish the bottom edge of the wolf skin. I remove wood around the little piece of hair, being careful not to cut it away too quickly.

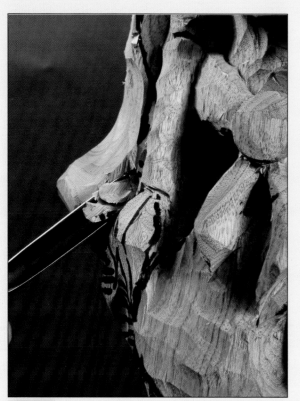

97 With a deep #11 (or #9) gouge, I separate the little piece of wolf skin sticking out in mid air, establishing another negative area.

98 In this photo, I have a large #8 gouge and I am "roughing up" the fur on the animal skin. That just gives it some preliminary texture; the cuts rough the skin up a little bit.

99 Here is another shot of me removing some waste and getting some of the wood out of the way.

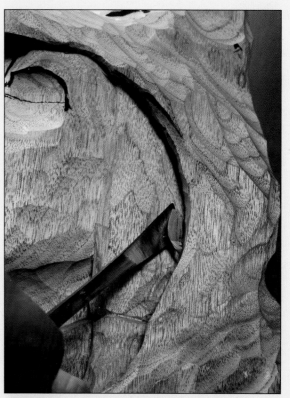

100 Using a small #3 fishtail gouge, I clean up the lines where the hair meets the wolf hide. I use the corners to get into the nooks and crannies to make nice clean cuts.

102 I make a final clean up around the neck to separate the neck, the hair and the scarf. Notice the angle of the knife. It is like a triangle cut. First I slice down the side of the neck, extending the neck back into the hair and down into the inside top of the scarf.

101 I use a V-tool to outline the bottom of the hair wraps, separating them from the tufts of hair that hang below. All along this stage I am roughing out, shaping areas down and getting everything set in so I can tell what the piece is going to look like. I have some beginning shapes: the hair wrappings have a "wrapped" look; the medallion on the scarf has a round, smooth look. All the shapes are there. Everything is looking good so far.

103 I am now attacking the piece from the other direction, cutting some wood away from the hair down around the outside of the scarf. Notice the angle of the knife.

104 I lay the knife on top of the scarf and slice in toward the neck to remove the big triangle shaving. It takes a little practice. Remember: wide angles. Don't put your knife in one way and then put it in at almost the same angle to relieve the piece. Open those angles up.

105 The pencil is pointing to where the hair goes into the top of the hair wrap. This is another area where you can use this triangle style cut to create a nice sharp, clean line. There are several areas where it works well, including cleaning up corners and in places where two or three things come together.

106 Now I've got everything blocked out on this carving and I know where everything is going to be. I have some preliminary textures and shapes in here and have defined them somewhat. Now I want to move back up to the face and work on it a little more. In this shot, I am using a #9 gouge and I am removing some wood from the bottom of the tip of the nose.

107 I use a wide #5 gouge to remove wood and take the mouth area back. First I take some wood off of the mouth area underneath the nose, that brings the tip of the nose out past the lips and the chin.

108 Notice the mouth area. This is what it should look like after you have removed the wood from underneath the nose. I am going to leave this area alone for now as I move up and start shaping the brow ridge to make it a little stronger.

109 Here you can see by the gouge cuts that I have scooped out a little wood around the eye sockets to define the brow ridge itself. Notice the shadow underneath the eye brow. I am using a #7, about 1/2 inch wide. That is a good brow-rounding tool. I round the brow in toward the center of the nose, using the gouge upside down.

110 With the same gouge, I come up the side of the nose and meet the cut to remove the chip. I want my cuts to look like the side that is completed. Notice the strong shadow on the inside of the brow.

111 Now I take a #11 (5 mm) gouge to create these deep gouge marks in the inside corner of the eye.

112 A #7 gouge is used to create the profile of the nose. (See diagrams A, B and C.) Notice in the picture that the arrows show the direction of the cut up to the bridge line. That's where the cut will stop.

113 Here's a shot of what the finished cut will look like. I've redrawn the centerline with a pencil.

114 I draw in the little flair at the end of the nose. It's shaved in a little bit, but mostly it is just drawn in so you can see how the flair is going to be positioned. Also notice the "hour glass" shape sketched on the edges of the nose cuts. This begins creating the "double diamond" shape. (See Diagram C.)

115 I take a larger #7 gouge, about 14 mm wide, and I make a couple of cuts in the direction of the arrows. These cuts create a double diamond effect, or the swelled area on the nose that narrows to the bridge of the nose. They also help to create a smooth transition from one shape to another with no sharp lines.

116 This is a shot of the finished cuts. You can see where the gouge marks are. You can also see how these cuts work together to shape the face.

117 On this photograph I've sketched in the nose, the eyemound area and the mouth. Take note of how the nose pulls back around the curve of the mouth.

118 I use a #7, 10 mm or 1/2 inch, to round off and set in the bottom of the nose. The cut is made right on the front on the tip of the nose. I round over, cutting straight into the face.

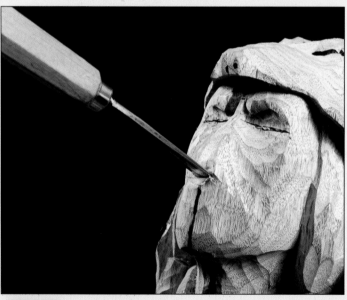

119 Here's another shot showing the angle of the tool as it goes into the face.

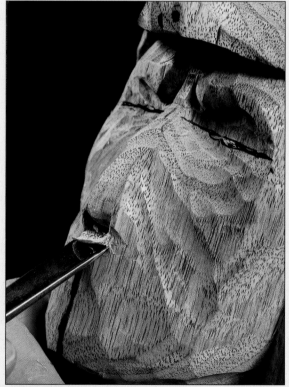

120 I take the same gouge and come up and meet the stop cut that I made over the end of the nose. This relieves some of the mouth area in that little trough that we have in the center of our upper lip.

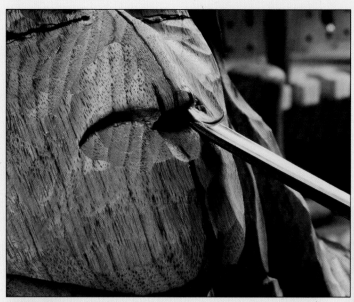

121 I make a stop cut to establish the bottom edge of the nose. I make the same cut on the opposite side of the face. I always do these cuts at the same time; it helps me to keep both sides of the nose even. A tip: Try to be as symmetrical as you can about your cuts.

122 With the same #7, I remove the wood up to the bottom of the nose.

123 Here I remove the wood up to the nose again. The two little marks on the end of the nose show where the cut starts. Those lines keep me from cutting that little center piece of the nose out or making the wood in that area too thin.

124 On the right side of this photo you can see a gouge cut marked with an arrow. That is the cut I'm making on the left side. These cuts help to establish the width of the nose.

126 In this shot from above, notice the angle of my tool. The arrow shows where the cut stops. This is very important. When I cut the wing of the nose in, I always cut at that outward angle, and I stop at the same angle. I don't roll the tool in behind the nose. That tends to bring the nose too far out on the face. I want the nose to fit in and around the mouth area.

125 Using the same #7, 10 mm, I make a cut from the tip of the nose back into the face at an outward angle. I turn the gouge over with the inside of the gouge toward the nose.

128 Remember that the tools I mention are just suggestions. Anything close to these will work. The most important thing is to use tools that you are familiar with and to achieve the same result. Here I am using a #9, 10 or 13 mm, to cut upward until I meet the cut that I made to establish the wing of the nose. The cuts have been completed on the right side of the photograph. On the left side of the photograph, the tool's coming up and removing the piece of wood.

127 Here's another shot of what the nose will look like after that cut is made. You can see where the corner of my tool has dug into the side of the nose. This shows where the cut starts and stops.

129 This is a shot of what the piece looks like after these gouge cuts are made. The cuts help to bring the nose back into the face. Sometimes, you may have to make these cuts a couple different times to get that nose pushed deep enough into the face.

130 Here's another view of what the piece looks like. Notice how the nose wraps around the dental curve and around the mouth area and goes back into the face. Getting this area correct is very important.

131 Notice the little ledge of wood on the mouth area. I've removed the wood to the centerline and stopped just to show you how much wood needs to come off and how far this area needs to be pushed back behind the tip of the nose.

132 Notice where the pencil is pointing. This is the area where the nostril cut stops before it reaches the back of the nose. It stops before it gets to where I made the wing of the nose. The wing cut rounds down underneath the nostril of the nose. (See Diagram D.)

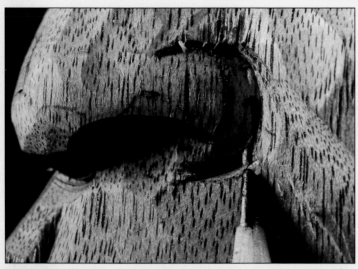

133 Here's a close-up view of the cuts.

134 I use a #11, 5 mm, to create the little gouge mark cut above the nostril. The cut blends down into the smile line.

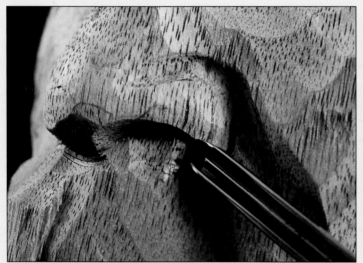

135 I use a #11, 3 mm, to dig out the nostril. I started where the nostril cuts stopped and started.

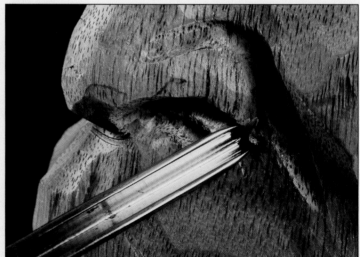

136 Here with the same small veinier, I'm coming underneath and hooking the wing of the nose up into the nostril. I continue my cut to wrap it right around the back of the nose.

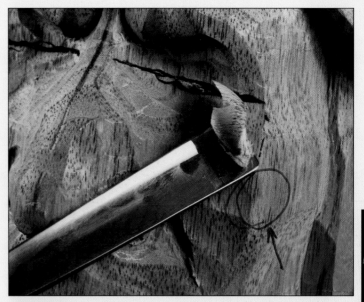

137 This close-up shows the finished nostril and nose. I now take a #3 or #2 gouge — any flat tool will work — and shave off the mouth area up to the nose. I want a smooth transition from the bottom of the nose down to the mouth area. I don't want a deep gouge cut in there, so I trim the mouth area back to the smile line that I've created.

138 OK. I've got the nose carved in. Now I want to pull the face back a little bit and refine the shapes around the eyes, the brow and the cheekbones. In this photo, I'm using a #5 to scoop out a little bit of wood underneath the eyes. I take off wood where the eyes are going to be and blend that area off the side of the nose and right off the side of the cheekbone. Notice from the arrow how this point of the cheekbone is underneath the outside corner of the eye.

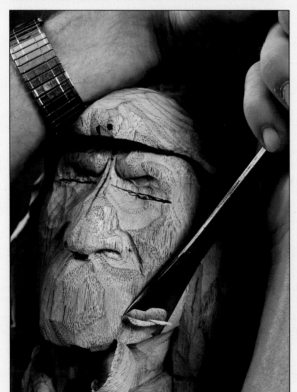

140 On this side view of the piece you can see the gouge cut.

139 I use a large #3 gouge to cut from the bottom of the cheekbone down and in toward the chin. I want to taper the chin and make the mouth area a little bit narrower.

141 Here's a front view of the face. I marked the center of the eyes. The mouth area is divided into three equal sections, and I've marked the width of the mouth. You'll notice the mouth is about as wide as the center of the eyes. On Indians, the mouth can be a little wider. As with anything, features vary from individual to individual.

142 Now I'm going to create a smile line using a V-tool. I start the cut where the tool is. This cut will establish the smile line. The mouth area has to work down to that line.

143 You can see the V-cut that created the smile line down around the corner of the mouth. I use a #3 gouge to shape the mouth area up to that wrinkle.

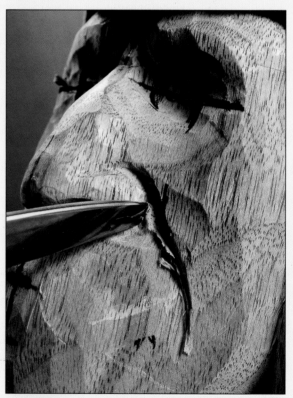

144 I need to deepen and define the smile line. I use a knife and take a little sliver of wood. A nice clean undercut — a good sharp line — is all I need. First I lay the knife point alongside the nose and push it deep into the face. Then I outline the round wing of the nose, cutting from the top to the bottom.

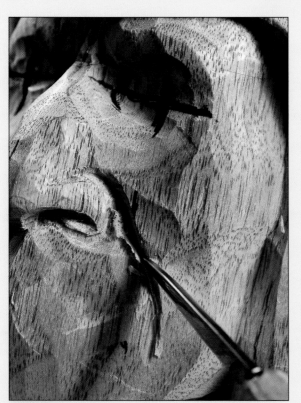

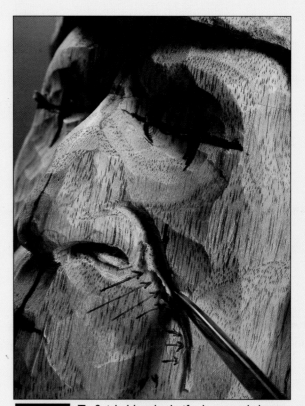

145 Next I take the knife and cut in at an angle to the face. I cut right down the smile line with the cut stopping just below, about at the corner of the mouth. The V-tool gave me a line to follow, yet I have a little room to change it if I need to.

146 To finish, I lay the knife down and shave right up to the smile line. This will remove that triangle or that sliver of wood. The arrows that you see in the picture show the direction of the cut.

147 On this front view, notice how the smile lines create a nice shadow. The face still appears a little chunky around the cheeks, but that will come. Everything constantly works down. After I get the mouth and the eyes in, I'll change some of that. (See Diagram E.)

148 I use a #11 gouge to remove a little bit of wood in front of that muscle right there at the corner of the mouth. I repeat this cut on the other side.

149 I shave the mouth area down to the muscle. This cut creates a kind of stair-step effect from the cheek to the muscle and then to the actual mouth area.

150 Next I'm going to cut the lips in. There are a couple of different ways you can do this. I like to use a wide angle V-tool and cut the lips in. Here I'm using a #11 or #9 gouge and cutting the lip in with the gouge first. This will create a separation and show me what the lips will look like before I actually V-tool them in.

151 Here you can see what the cut looks like. Notice the muscle area at the corner of the mouth.

152 I want to separate the chin from the bottom lip by making a gouge cut from the center right on down over the jaw line. I am using a large #11. A #11, 10 mm, or a #9 will work well.

153 As you can see in this photograph, I've softened up some of the areas and trimmed down the chin a little bit. I want to push the face back and get it adjusted. Throughout the carving process, as I carve one part of the face, I have to push the rest of the face back accordingly. This helps to give a good, strong appearance, instead of getting a face that seems too flat.

154 I round off the chin a little bit, softening up some of those sharp edges. Everything needs to be a smooth transition.

155 Here I am using that wide angle V-tool again. I draw a line in to where I want to cut. I usually start at the center and work out to each corner on both sides.

156 Now that I have finished with the V-tool, this is what the piece looks like. I still need to give the lips a little bit of shape and round them over, so that the plane of the lip isn't flat.

157 Here's another shot of the face. You can see how everything fits in the mouth area in comparison with the rest of the face.

158 To round the lips, I use a #7 gouge. A #5 or a #3 will also work well as long as the tool is not too flat. I flip the tool upside-down and work from the center to the corners on the top.

159 I do the same thing to the top of the lips. Now, once I get them rounded over, I have to establish the edge where the pink of the lip meets the skin.

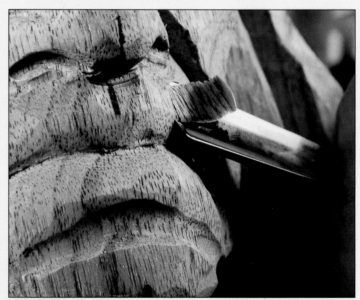

160 You can see what the lips look like when they are rounded off. The cuts make them look really fat. I can leave them this way, or I can choose to thin them down. To establish that edge, I'll take the #7 and make a cut right along the top of the lip where the tool is. I start at the corner and cut from the corner up to the center.

161 I make the same cut on the bottom. One thing to remember when carving lips: The bottom lip tucks underneath the top lip at the outside corners. Because of this, I start at the center, cutting to the corners on the bottom.

162 This is where the tool ends up. Notice how you can see the edge of the lips now, and how they've got some form to them. I pause here to clean up and check my lines. I want to make sure everything is as even as it possibly can be.

163 I take a #11 gouge and strengthen the line between the bottom lip and the chin. That separation there is also important to the character of the piece.

164 Here, right underneath the nose, I am creating that little dent that runs between the nose and the top lip. I use a #11 gouge to make this cut.

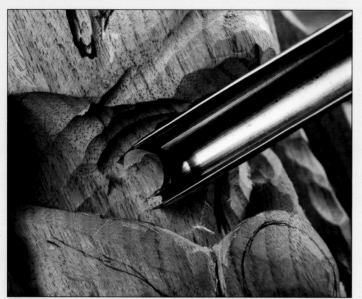

165 Here I am using a #8 or a #9 gouge. I like to use these to create the cut from the chin down toward the inside of the scarf. Sometimes a #7 works well, if I've got a little more room. Now I need to visualize the neck. The windpipe, or the esophagus tube, comes down the center of the neck, and there are muscles on each side. There is a little hollow on each side as well, and then the neck spreads out back behind the jaw.

166 Here you can see what the neck looks like after blending in the cuts. Notice some of the shapes the cuts have created on the neck.

167 This photo is the same as the previous shot. I have labeled some areas of note. Section one is the Adam's apple area and the little narrow tube that goes right down the center of the neck. Notice how it blends off the bottom of the chin. The curved line is a deep gouge cut. I left a ledge of wood right under the chin to show you how much wood has to come off the neck. Section two is the hollow area. Notice how it blends off the separation line from the chin and lip above. The third area is the widest part of the neck back under the jaw. (See Diagram F.)

168 I use a knife to make a sharp cut that will separate the lips a little bit. Notice the other things that are going on here. Take a look at the nostril, the smile line, the profile line that comes down around the corner of the mouth, and the little area at the end of the line where the muscle is. Also notice the transition on the muscle under the corner of the bottom lip between the lip and the chin. Now take another look and notice how all these things come together.

169 I use a V-tool to sharpen the separation between the bottom lip and the chin. I make the cut right up on top of the chin area. I don't want to carry it all the way down into the neck; I just want to keep it right here in the center. This cut will give the lower lip a little sharper shadow.

170 Now I am working on the chin, smoothing it off and rounding it. You can see what the V-cut between the lip and the chin looks like. There are two muscles right on the point of the chin and a little dent in the center. Setting the #3 in the center of the chin and twisting it a little bit will create a cleft right there.

171 The face was a little bit chunky a while ago. Now I'm going to give the piece a kind of hungry look. I want to make the shapes of the face a little narrower and skinnier. I use a #8 gouge to create a hollow in the cheek and underneath the point of the cheek bone. I usually cut down behind the muscles around the mouth. This creates the hollow in the cheek with which we're all familiar.

172 Here's an overview of the piece to this point. The neck is pretty well finalized, and all the face shapes are in. The hair masses, the hair wraps and the scarf around the neck and the bolo are all blocked in. I've drawn in some of the wrinkles. The overall outer shape of the carving is there, as are the negative spaces.

173 To begin work on the eyes, I start with a #11, 5 mm. I cut in from the top, working on the inside corner. I already carved these in here to show you the effect you're looking for and how to use the tool. (See Diagrams G and H.)

174 The first cut is from the top down to the center. The second is from the bottom up to the center.

175 Here you can see the angle that I am using with the tool.

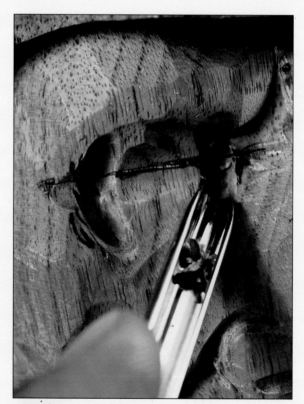

176 The arrows here show the direction of the cuts. Notice the center line is just below the little wrinkle on the top of the nose.

177 Now I am going to do the same to the outside corner. I cut in from the top, then down to the center.

178 I cut from the bottom up to the center.

179 I take the same gouge and cut out the outside corner. This helps wrap the bone outlining the socket around the corner of the skull and allows the eye to "get out," so to speak.

180 Here is a side view close-up of what the piece looks like so far. Notice how the front of the eyeball area is fairly straight up and down. Notice the deep cuts in the corner and the shape of the orbit around the eye. I've rounded the edges off a little bit and darkened the corners of the eye mound so that I can see what I have to round off.

181 A different view of the same area shows the depth of these cuts. These corners need to be pushed far back in there. This will give me a nice round mound from side to side.

182 Notice the depth from the front of the nose back to the corner, and notice that the plane on the front of the eyeball is straight up and down. It's important not to let the bottom area below the center line of the eye to stick out farther than the top area.

183 Here's an overall shot of the piece with the deep corners created around the eye mounds. You can see how it looks like a square chunk in there with corners on it.

184 In this close-up shot, notice the depth and how I stayed out away from the bridge of the nose. I stop here and check that the widths of the eye mounds are the same. I want to keep them symmetrical at this point.

185 I use a #8 or a #9 5mm gouge — anything narrow that will round the corners of that mound — will work too. Notice, I'm not cutting away in the center part of the eye. I'm working from the center down to the corner in a rounding motion. I am trying to make this area in there look like a cylinder.

186 Here's another shot of the rounded mounds. Notice I've drawn my centerlines back in across the center. The middle of the eye is still marked. I still haven't cut any wood off there yet. This keeps the height in the middle of the eye and creates the roundness from side to side that is so important. (See Diagrams J, K and L.)

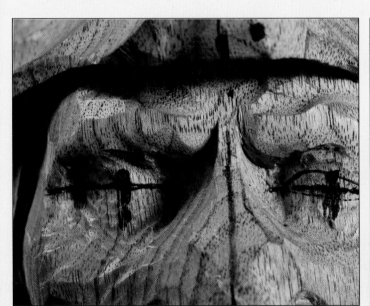

187 I have drawn in the eye shape on the photograph. Notice how the inside corner of the eye starts out away from the nose a little bit. In this photograph you can see how the eyelids fit on the mound.

188 I cut in the top eyelid with a knife. I just cut straight in, making a nice, clean, sharp stopcut. I left the center marks up and down in the middle of the eyes to show where the highest point of the eye is located.

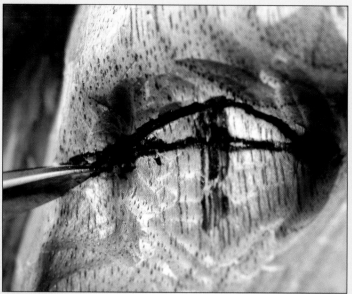

189 Notice how the outside corner of the eyelid drops below the center mark.

190 I now shave up to the top eyelid to the stopcut. This step is probably one of the most important steps in completing the eye. Notice how I'm holding the knife, and how low I am starting on the eyeball area. On the other side I've drawn little arrows showing about where I start the cut.

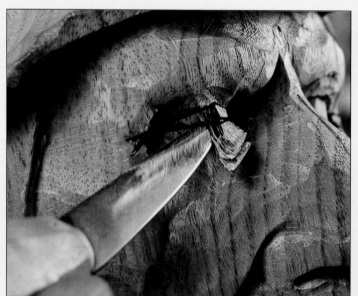

191 Here's another shot of the cut. While I'm working on this top eyelid, I want to maintain a round appearance. It's important to keep the roundness from side to side that I established earlier. The thickness of the eyelid will be the same from corner to corner. If it gets too thick in the middle, chances are the eyeball has probably flattened out too much.

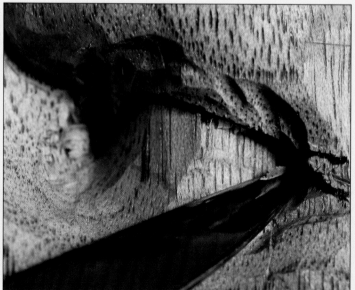

192 You can see the end of my centerline and where the top eyelid drops below the centerline a little bit. I use the point of a knife or a little #11 gouge to hook out the outside corner of that eye. I always extend my centerline up the inside corner of the nose and out the outside corner of the eye, as you can see here. Without these marks the tendency is to redraw the centerline in a lower position, which will make the eyes appear too wide open, not squinty like I want them to be.

193 This is a profile view of what this area should look like. Notice how part of the centerline comes out on the side of the head a little bit. Also, notice the top lid area and the brow ridge, and how the plane of the front of the eye is straight up and down.

194 Here is a closer shot. As you can see, this is the area that should be straight up and down. I can't stress the importance of this enough. The bottom part of the eye can't stick out farther than the top part. If that happens and the eye starts to look a little "buggy," just remove some wood from below the centerline to straighten it back up.

195 A shot from the front gives another perspective on the piece. Notice the positioning of the centerline.

196 Here's the same shot with the bottom eyelids drawn in. Notice how that bottom eyelid is kept close to the centerline. The top eyelid acts like a shutter over the eyeball and moves up and down; the bottom eyelid just stays put, like a stop.

197 I now use a knife to make a stopcut right along the bottom eyelid. In this case, I usually try to cut from the inside corner to the center, almost to the outside corner, and then stop. Otherwise, too much pressure will chip the eyeball on either corner.

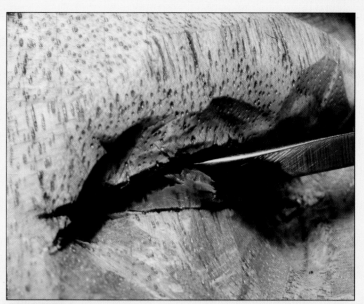

198 From here on, I cut from the top eyelid <u>down</u> to the bottom eyelid, <u>never</u> cutting up again. I'm using a little 2 mm skew chisel here, but a knife will also work well. I put the chisel right in at the top eyelid and slice down.

199 Now the eye's in there. This is what the inward angle should look like from the side view.

200 Sometimes this area can bulge out too far. If necessary, remove a little wood here.

201 With a #9, 5 mm gouge, I clean off the bag of the eye. I lay in some basic ripple lines with this gouge first to prepare the area for those little, fine wrinkles that will come later. I follow a pattern of three basic lines. (See Diagram M.)

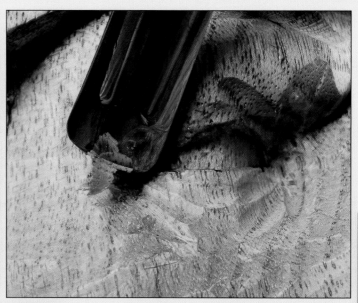

202 Here I am using a #5 or a #7 gouge, about a half-inch wide, to reround the brow area and the orbit around the eye. You can see a little of the wrinkle cuts that I made underneath the eye. They follow the wrinkle pattern of the face.

203 I use a #8, 3 mm gouge to mark the pupil. Notice how I am going straight in and then at a little bit of a downward and outward angle from the pupil. I don't cut in and up underneath the pupil. I always want to have pressure going away from that little pupil in there.

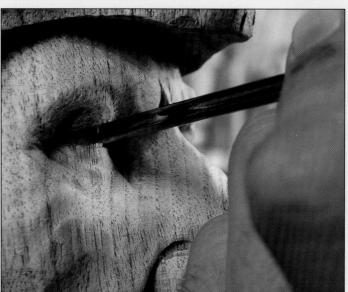

204 Notice the downward angle of the tool in relationship to the front of the eye. This is just like carving a button on a shirt. I rotate the tool just to meet the top of the eyelid. This creates that button in there. Again, I always cut on a downward and outward angle away from the pupil.

205 Again, I just apply a little bit of pressure and twist the tool in. All the pressure goes away from the pupil, not up behind it. This way the pupil gradually gets a little wider and bigger as I cut deeper.

206 You can see a slight line where I cut the original pupil. I outline and start to remove the iris, or the colored part of the eye, from the pupil with a #8, 3 mm gouge. This is the big, thick cut that you see. I use a knife to remove a crescent shaped chip. With these kind of eyes, I am basically leaving the pupil and the white area and cutting out the colored part.

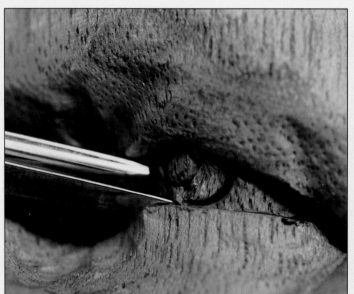

207 Here I am removing the iris on the other side. This is how I establish that cut to start to remove the iris. Then I relieve the chip at the top eyelid with a knife.

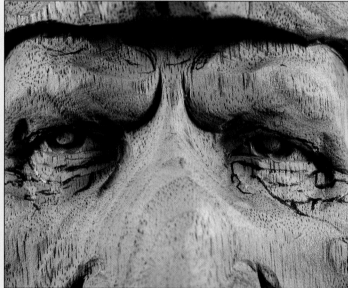

208 This is what the eye looks like when I'm done. See how the pupil and the whites of the eye remain; the colored part, the iris, is gone. I now draw in the fine wrinkle pattern around the eye. I also draw a few wrinkles on the forehead to follow the structure around the brow and create a stronger facial expression. Notice how the bottom eyelid tucks up in underneath the top eyelid on the outside corners.

209 I use a #11, 3 or 4 mm gouge to trace the wrinkle lines that I drew on the face.

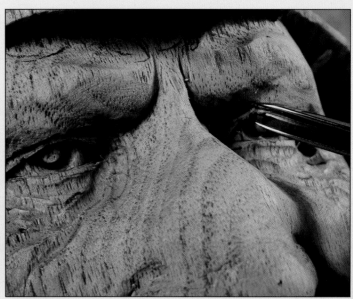

210 The left eyelid has already been cut in with the veiner. On the right hand side of the photo, I'm using a little veiner to cut the lid in on the top. I remove just a little sliver of wood. My tool needs to be extremely sharp or it will crumble the eyelids.

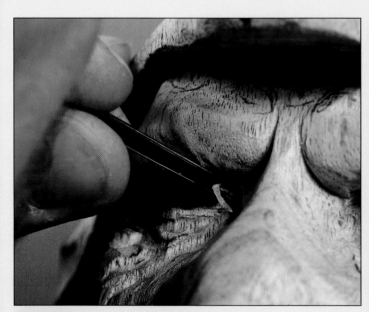

211 Now I need to sharpen the wrinkles. I use a very small V tool, a 1 or 2 mm or maybe even a 3 mm. I retrace the cuts I made with the gouge. I don't cut real deep. All I want is a nice, sharp, little line.

212 I am finished with one side and am now working on the other side. Notice how the nose and the face look smooth, like they've been sanded. I use a product called Scotch Brite to soften and smooth the wood so it looks like skin and bone and muscle. After I carve the wrinkles, I use Scotch Brite, just lightly, around the eye. That will soften all those wrinkles and make them look like creases in the skin.

213 Both eyes are finished, the wrinkles are in, and all I have left to do is soften some of the sharp edges and blend the areas together. Notice the position of the Indian's pupils. He appears to be looking a little bit over your left shoulder. I never center pupils. It gives the piece too much of a vacant stare.

214 A photograph from the front shows the progress to this point.

215 I turn the piece sideways and study the Indian's profile. I look closely at the eyes, the bridge of the nose, the mouth, the neck and the shape of the wolf headdress. If I need to make any adjustments, now is the time to do it.

216 Here you can see all the cuts and how the bag and the wrinkles lay in under the eye. You'll also notice the face is a little bit rough now. I use the coarse brown Scotch Brite to smooth out those little corners around every V cut, but a little flat chisel will work well too.

217 Here I have used the Scotch Brite on the face. You can see how much softer everything looks. The wood appears a little more natural and more like creased skin. All the pencil marks are gone and the transitions are very smooth.

218 I am now ready to begin work on the wolf headdress. First I want to break up this large mass of wood. I use a large #11, 15 mm gouge to lay in some rough texture.

219 Here I am using a smaller #11, 7 mm to put in the fur. This is about as fine as I texture the fur in this area. I use S cuts, curved cuts and U cuts — nothing straight. I make sure to follow the pattern of the animal's natural hair tracts when I'm putting in the fur. I treat the head a little differently. The hair on the nose, around the eyes and on the ears is finer than the rest of the animal's fur. I want a smooth transition from the coarse fur to the finer fur.

220 I draw a pattern of the hair as it grows around the face right on the wood with a black marker. Then I begin to texture the hair with a #9, 5 mm gouge.

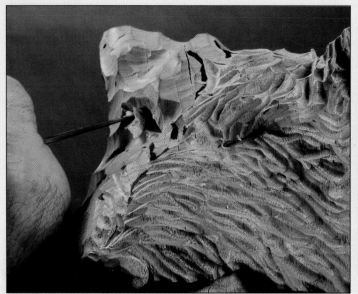

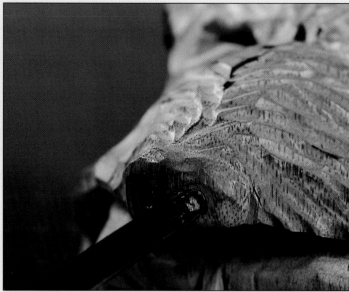

221 Here you can see what the texture looks like. You can also see a line where the finer texture meets the rougher texture on the side of the animal's head. I'll smooth that out a little more later. Here I am working on the eyes. One eye has already been cut in. I am now cutting on the other eye with a knife. Notice how the fur rolls into the eye slit.

222 Before I start on the nose, I take a look at my dog's nose for a model. I first use a #11, 3 mm to pop a little circle out for the nose hole.

223 I round the wing around the nostril up into the nostril opening with a small #7 gouge. The other side has already been completed.

224 When I finish with the wolf headdress, I'm ready to work on the hair around the Indian's face and neck. Here I'm using a #8 gouge to give the area a little bit of big, bold texture. It's always a good idea to break that mass into some smaller sections and separate it a little more before I actually texture the hair itself.

225 You can see that I've divided the area into three sections. Notice how it all appears to pull down into the top of the tie. That just adds to the effect. The next step is to actually texture the hair.

226 In this photo I'm using a #11, 5 mm gouge to put in the hair. The grain is kind of tricky here. I find that long, sweeping strokes from the bottom to the top work best. I tuck the cuts in the tie. Remember to keep the cuts flowing so that they look more like real hair.

227 Here I am texturing the little tuft of hair that hangs below the tie. On the end of the tuft I use the same #11 gouge to separate and texture the hair.

228 The hair wraps are done with a square angle V-tool to keep them flat and to give them that wrapped look. I lay the tool on its side and make stairsteps right down to the bottom.

229 Now I move on to the scarf. It's a cloth scarf that has a bolo type ring with a little medallion on the front. I want it to look wrinkled and pulled, rolled and twisted—like a neckerchief does when you tie it around your neck. I lay in some basic wrinkles with a #11 or #9, 7 mm gouge.

230 Next, I blend in some of the edges and clean up the area. Then I take a small #11, 3 mm gouge to better define the little wrinkles and folds, getting deeper toward the bolo.

231 I define and sharpen the cuts in the scarf even more. I want to create some shadow and some interest. I use a little V tool and cut down through the same cut I made with the veinier. Here in the photo, I'm using a knife to take out just a tiny little sliver to show some depth in these wrinkles and cracks.

232 I am now ready to move on to the bolo. Any design will do. First I draw in the circle within the button. Then I take a small V-tool, a 2 or 3 mm, and outline the circle.

233 I use a small #5 gouge to clean off the rim around the button.

234 As you can see here, I lower the rim a little bit and recess it back. I use a #5 gouge to texture the center of the button. I remove a bunch of tiny chips all over it to give it the look of beat-out, dented metal.

235 I move on to the bottom ties on the scarf. I want to create some movement and some twisting on the ends of the scarf. I use a #7 gouge, about a half-inch wide, to make a twisting cut. I start at one side and roll over the contour of the ties.

236 Here I am creating the bottom edge of the scarf. I want to raise it up off the wolf cape and leave the tip to flare out. I use the same tool to cut out some wood underneath the scarf. I let the shape of the tool dictate the shape of the cuts.

237 Here is a photograph of the finished scarf end. I deepened the little wrinkles and created a flared-in edge around the cloth to mark the edge of the scarf. I used a v-tool to make a puckered little wrinkle where the scarf goes up into the medallion.

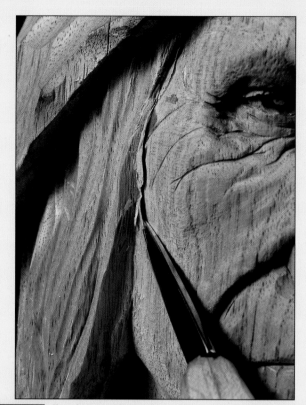

238 I'm done with the face, done with the hair and almost done with the wolf headdress, the neck and the scarf area. Now it's time to separate these areas from each other. For example, I want to separate the hair from the face. To do that I need to create an undercut. I ask myself, what goes back underneath what. In this case, the face goes back underneath the hair. I take the knife and I extend the face back into the hair straight back parallel to the face.

239 Using a knife, I remove wood away from the hair. This creates the under cut. Compare the angle of the knife in this photograph with the angle of the knife in the previous photo. That's a wide open angle. All I want is a nice clean sharp line; the whole chip will fall out by itself. Remember: Like anything else, this takes a little practice and a good sharp knife.

240 In this photo, notice the hair that goes down in underneath the robe and the tip of the hair that hangs below the edge of the robe. Those two are part of the same bunch of hair. As you can see in the photograph, the tassel at the bottom is farther out toward the front than the hair at the top and the wrap. I need to adjust that accordingly to get this area of the piece finished up.

241 From left to right, these are the bits that I use: I cut the Scotch Brite pads in about 1 1/2 inch squares and put them on this mandrel in a Foredom. Next are two carver's drills. These bits are very sharp and aggressive. I use them to grind out the nose. Next is a flame burr for the eyes. Finally a little diamond disc used to texture fine hair or fur.

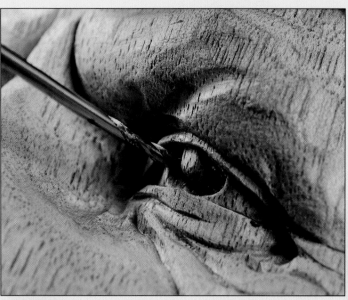

242 With a regular drill bit, I drill a pilot hole on both sides of the pupil. The bit must be small enough to fit between the pupil and the edge of the iris, or cut-out part, because I don't want to damage either part of the eye. I just want to grind out the part that I already cut out.

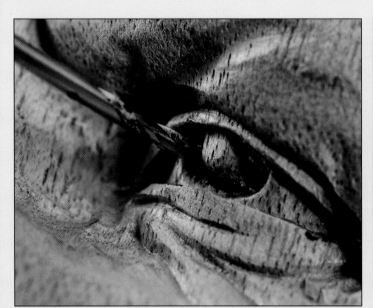

243 You can see in this photograph where that bit starts. I set it in before I start it and take my time. It's important to be patient and very, very careful.

244 Notice in this view how long this bit is. The longer the better. I drill back as far as I can. This gives me two pilot holes to follow when I'm hollowing out the wood behind the eyes. (See Diagram P.)

245 Notice again how far in I'm drilling. I need to be careful not to let my handpiece hit the carving. Always drill straight into the piece.

246 While I have this bit in, I move up to the headdress and drill out the wolf's nostrils. This is also a good time to drill the holes for the Indian's nostrils too. I drill at a slight upward angle as far back as I can. This creates a pilot hole, and that's all I'm concerned with right now. I want to drill in deep enough that I can find the holes when I hollow out the back.

247 Moving back to the eyes, I put a flame burr in the handpiece. See the little holes I drilled on each side of that pupil? I start the flame burr in that hole and start to grind out the iris area.

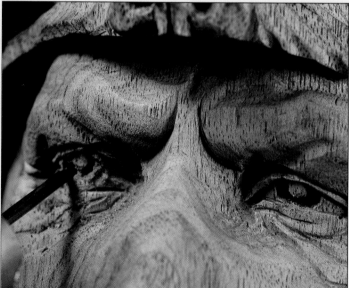

248 I grind out the area, being careful not to disfigure the edges of my cuts or the pupil. The eye on the right hand side is finished; I am working on the left side.

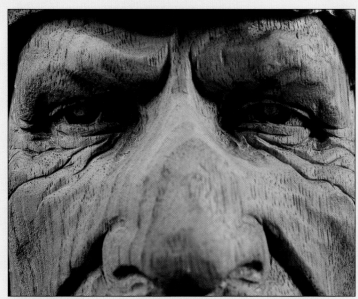

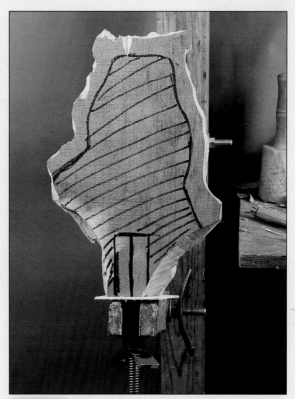

249 Here is a shot of the eyes from the front. It creates a dramatic dark effect. There is more of a shadow now than before we ground out the eyes. This effect is also one of the things I like about masks.

250 OK... Now I'm ready to begin to hollow out some wood on the back of the piece. The carving has to be pretty well finished from the front before I start to hollow out the back. That's important. The front is what tells me how much I have to take off in the back. I mark off at least a one inch edge all the way around the carving. Notice the square I've drawn at the bottom with the line through it. That's where the screw is. Keeping that block there will allow me to finish this whole carving while it's mounted.

251 To drill out the nostrils, I use the small carver's drill bit in the Foredom. This is the point where I start drilling.

252 The nice thing about these particular bits is that I can cut sideways with them. I just drill in, proceeding slowly and carefully.

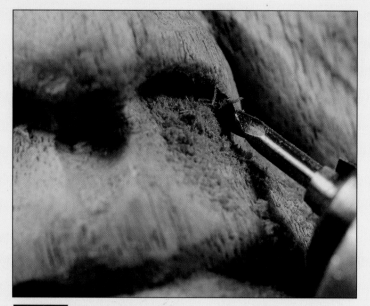

253 I swing the bit around to wind up here.

254 Turning the piece over to the back, you can see how the hollowing out has progressed. At this point, I'm all done hollowing out the back. If you study the picture you'll get an idea of how much wood I removed. I try to keep about a one inch width of wood around the outer edge.

255 These circled areas show where the eye holes and the nose holes come through the back of the piece. Remember the pilot holes that I put in with the drill? You can see now how I find them as I hollow out the back. They give me a guide to follow so I don't make the face, and everything else, too thin.

256 In this close up shot of the back, you can see the amount of wood I've hollowed out. I use a couple of long bent gouges and a couple of spoon gouges when I get down closer and closer to the backs of the eyes and the nose.

257 Here you can see just how much has to come off of the back. This is pretty well done. I've removed everything that shouldn't be there.

258 A shot taken from the other side of the shoulder shows you how I treated that area.

259 In this profile shot, notice how I left the big chunk of wood on the bottom in the back where that screw is. Everything else is gone. You can almost see where I am going to cut off that chunk.

260 Here's a view from the front. Did you notice that I switched carvings on you? This particular piece has a little bit different treatments of the necklace and the hair wraps. These are just some various ideas that you can work into your piece. I used the little diamond disc to create the texture on the hair ties.

261 Turning the piece over again, you can see how I hollow out the wood behind the eyes and the nose. I use a black marker to isolate the area and then continue to remove just the wood behind the eyes and the nose.

262 Get the wood in these areas as thin as you can. I know this is not a part of the carving that shows, but I don't want it to be sloppy or fuzzy or messy. Take a close look at the hole behind the eye on the top right of the photograph. You can see all the way through the mask to the wall behind.

263 I turn the carving back around to the front to check the eyes. Notice how the eyes are hollowed out and what they look like with light behind them.

264 Here you can see the chunk of wood that holds the carving to the screw. The black line shows where the screw is probably located. I take one more look at the carving to make sure I'm done and happy with everything. Then I just pull the screw out.

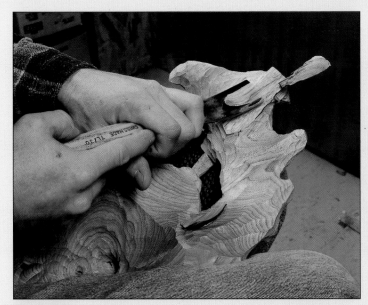

265 I hold the carving between my knees with the chunk of wood sticking out away from my leg. I carefully remove that square chunk of wood with a big gouge and clean off the back side.

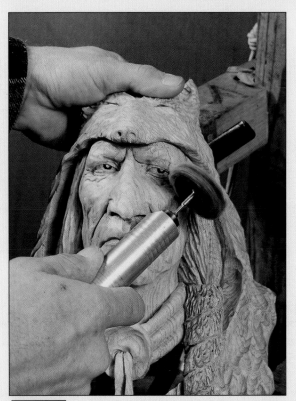

266 I put a Scotch Brite pad in the mandrel and work the whole carving. I sculpt the face a little bit, smooth it off and blend in the areas to make it look like skin and muscle. The Scotch Brite helps to remove some of the tool marks and dust and chips. Once I've used Scotch Brite on the entire piece, I'm ready to stain it up.

267 Here's a shot of the various products I use to stain this piece. Bartley's Gel Varnish is a pudding-consistency product that is thinned down in a jar. As you can see, it has an amber color and creates a very nice finish that doesn't affect basswood or butternut. I use oil paints to add color. The two cans are dark and natural Watco Satin Finishing Wax.

268 I use an oil-based finish. The base product is Bartley's Gel Varnish. I've used other products, but this one is my current favorite.

269 To start, I thin the varnish down with paint thinner, mineral spirits or turpentine until it reaches the consistency of linseed oil or a little bit thinner.

270 I apply this varnish mixture to the entire piece and also use this mixutre as a vehicle for the oil color.

271 Here is the expensive pallet that I use. A simple piece of cardboard seems to serve the purpose. I mix up a gray base coat, a little on the lighter side than on the dark side, using Mars black and Titanium white. You may opt for a different color here. When it comes to painting the wolf skin, the best thing to do is to study some pictures of the live animal.

272 I add the gray color to the whole wolf skin area and to the fur on the wolf. There's quite a large area to cover, so I make a very thin stain out of the varnish mixture and the gray color that I mixed up.

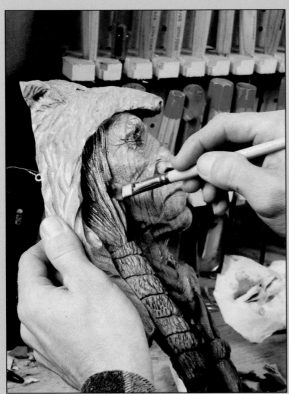

273 In this next series of photos, I add black to the hair. This is basically a tinting or a staining process, not necessarily painting, because you can still see the wood through the color.

274 Next I add some Titanium white highlights around the eye area and along the edge of the wolf skin to lighten it up when compared to the gray. The piece is wet with the varnish, and I add the color while the varnish is wet. This way everything stays very workable and I can blend colors very well. That's one reason why I like oil paints.

275 I add black highlights and markings to the wolf's skin. I make some gray areas and darken other areas. I want to keep the contrast from the black to the white strong yet blended. Everything's got to blend together but yet have some distinctions in the markings.

276 When the markings are to my liking, I paint the nose of the wolf black.

277 Here is a close-up of the painted face. The bone pipes are white with some highlights. Shadows were created using burnt umber oil paint. Anywhere there was a natural shadow, I added a shadow. On this piece, the left half is shadowed.

278 I let my piece dry at least overnight or until it's not tacky anymore. It usually takes overnight depending on the humidity.

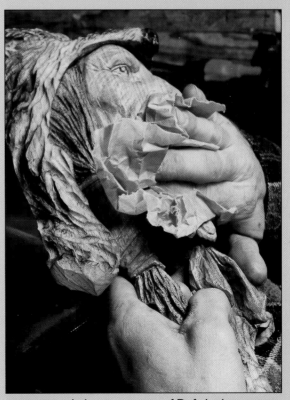

279 After the piece dries, I give it at least one and no more than three coats of Deft Semi-Gloss Spray. I don't want to soak my piece. Light coats are better than one heavy coat. (Because of the time factor in shooting this book, we're using a combination of both pieces in this section.)

280 In between coats of Deft, I take a crumpled-up brown paper sack and rub the piece down. This acts as a very light abrasive. It helps to smooth the piece off a little bit from the Deft.

281 Here's the piece after it's been sprayed and rubbed down with a paper sack. You can see how the Deft leaves a slight shine when it dries.

282 After I'm finished, I brush the sack dust off with a dry clean paint brush or an air compressor. I spray the piece with Krylon Matte Spray, number 1311. The Krylon dulls any shine left by the Deft.

283 I use only a light coat of Krylon Matte Spray. The Krylon usually dries within 30 minutes or less.

284 All that's left now is to wax the piece. I use Watco Satin Finishing Wax. There's a dark finish and a natural, which is clear. I use a mixture of the two: One part dark to three parts clear. This tends to make a softer brown wax instead of such a dark blacker wax.

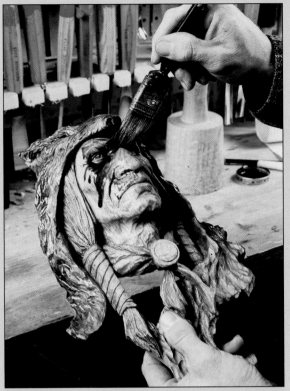

285 Notice how I flood the piece with the wax. I let it soak down and bleed into all the cracks and crevices and nooks and crannies.

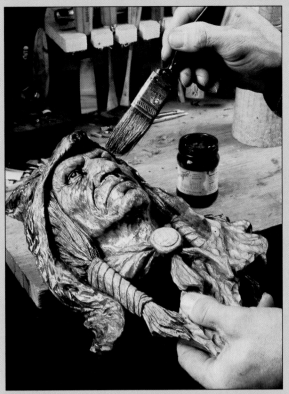

286 Watco Satin Finishing Wax is a liquid. Therefore, it antiques and waxes the piece all in one step, which can be a real time-saver.

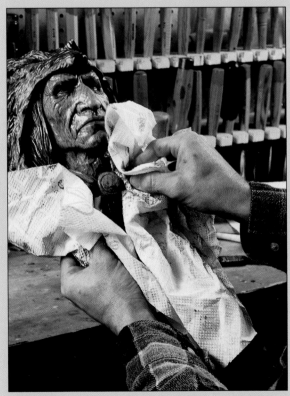

287 I let the piece sit for several minutes, then I use a paper towel to wipe the excess off the piece. I don't want the wax to puddle up anywhere. After I wipe the excess off, I set the piece up to dry.

288 When the wax is dry, which usually takes 30 minutes to an hour, I buff the piece. (If you don't get around to buffing it for a couple of weeks, it won't hurt it.) I use a brush in an electric drill. This saves a lot of effort and does a fine job. I haven't found this particular brush available anymore, but there are several brushes out there on the market that will do a nice job.

289 I buff my carving until the wax leaves a nice shine. This is the finish I use on almost all of my carvings.

290 Here is the finished carving. I hope you've enjoyed working with this piece. Feel free to improvise on any aspect of the design or the carving. Use your imagination. That's what this is all about, after all.

291 Here's a shot of three finished examples. The first two are completely finished and waxed. The last one has not been sealed or waxed yet so you can see the difference that the wax creates.

Options

To write this book, I actually made two carvings of Indians in wolf headdresses. The carving in the main how-to demonstration sports a scarf and bolo. The necklace and the hair wraps were treated a little differently on the second piece. In this section, let's take a closer look at the second carving and some other options. You may want to use some of these elements to give your next carving a different look.

Front.

Profile.

Necklace.

Hair wrap.

Hair wrap.

Bolo and scarf.

A tied bandanna is another option you can use at the Indian's neck. Of course, the best way to learn how to carve a tied bandanna is to tie one to look at. A good model is a great starting point. Here are some step-by-step pointers to carving a knot.

I draw the scarf on a block of wood. With a black marker, I outline the entire mask. I want to set up the mask first to make sure the scarf will look right.

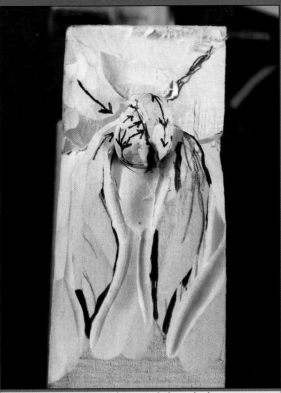

I start removing wood around the whole mass, getting it brought up. Then I isolate wood for the knot, the two ends of the bandanna that are hanging down, and the material that goes on around the neck.

Here's a close-up of the knot. Notice how I had to create levels to make it look like the scarf is tied.

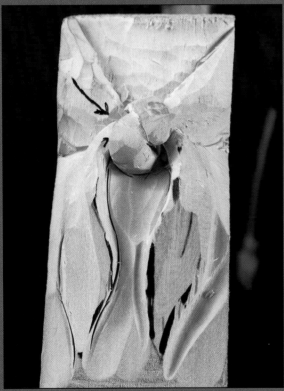

This is another shot of the whole knot process. the arrow shows the direction of the scarf where it puckers to go into the knot.

And finally, here's the finished knot. As with anything, carving knots takes some practice. The trick to doing something new like this is to look at a model and break it down into depths and levels and shapes and then refine it to the finished product.

Common Problems

This next section covers some common problems that occur when carving eyes and noses. I've found that sometimes the best way to teach a correct method is to show something that was done incorrectly. And that's exactly what I'm going to do here. This piece is one of my earlier carvings, and it's a prime example of the mistakes that do happen. Everyone has to start somewhere — including myself — so I'm not ashamed to share this piece with you.

Here's a front view of the subject I'm going to use as an example. Take a look at the eyes and the nose. Notice the severe angle of the far eye and how it is sloping back into the head.

In this profile view, you can again see the backward angle of the eye. You can also see how the entire nose is hanging off the front of the face.

Looking at this shot, I've drawn a couple of lines to show the angle of the eye and how much of the nose is hanging off of the face. The face is shallow in behind the nose.

Most of these problems happen during the preliminary carving stages, and now is the time to fix them. Let's take a closer look.

This is how you attempt to fix the problem. Take some wood off below the centerline and push the bottom half of the eye back so that the profile of the eye is straight up and down.

Here you can see the finished, corrected eye. Notice the shape and the angle at which it is sitting in the mound for the eye. The angle is pretty much straight up and down now and that's how you want it to be. Following the steps for carving the eye in the how-to section of this book and reviewing this section should help to eliminate any problems you have getting the initial shape of the eye in the head at the correct angle.

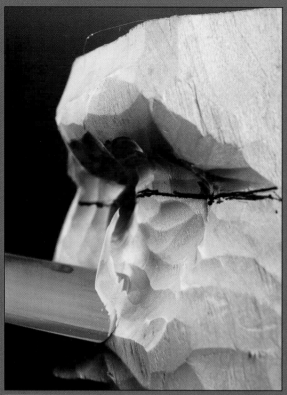

Now, let's see how we can create a better nose. You can see by the eye how I removed a lot of wood below the centerline. Here I am pushing the cheek back to get it underneath the eye.

In this photo, the eye has been corrected and the cheek has been pushed back. That smooth transition of form from the nose to the cheek has been created and blended a little bit better. You now can see how I begin the nose. The lines that are drawn show how much of the nose is hanging off the face and how much should be pushed into the face.

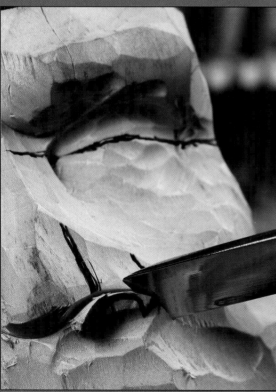

First I establish the bottom center of the nose. Then I establish the bottom edge of the nostril. This point is where the nose starts to go back into the face.

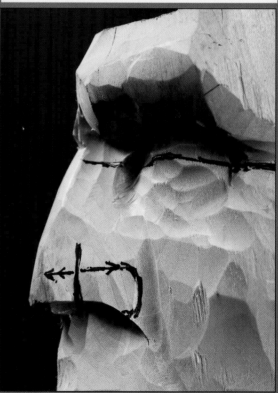

These lines show the amount of the nose that's hanging off the face and the amount that pushes into the face. You can see about how far to cut the wing of the nose.

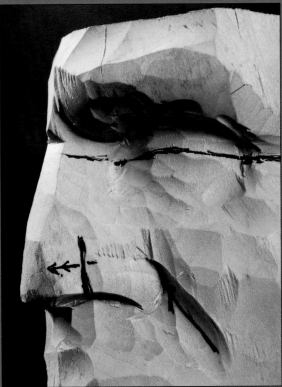

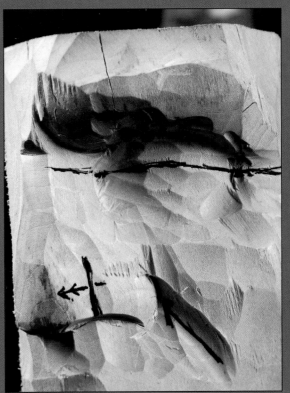

Now I cut the wing in. Notice the positive, or rounded, shape that has been created there. Also notice that it has been pushed back into the face. Look at the distance from the straight line on the side of the nose to the smile line. You'll notice an arrow has been drawn on the smile line. That shows the direction of the cut that makes the shadow line.

Here's a different angle of the whole area completed.

This shot, taken from underneath the nose, shows you the shape of the nose and how it wraps back around that dental curve on the face. Again, combining this information with the step-by-step information in the how-to section should help clear up a few common problems.

Diagram 1 - *Face Shapes*

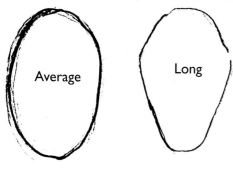

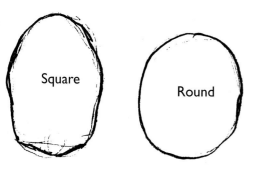

Average

Long

Square

Round

Diagram 2 - *General Geometric Shaping*

Learn to establish planes, especially when roughing out a piece from a block. Here you can see how the wolf headdress was reduced to geometric shapes.

Diagram 3 - *Arcs and Curves*

A typical bust or mask utilizes a triangle base. This basic base can be made more interesting by adding a C-curve or an S-curve.

Diagram 4 - *Profiles*

A profile on a mask is primarily to study and familiarize yourself with your idea.

Diagram 5 - *Sketches*

Sketches of your ideas will help you refine your ideas.

Diagram 6 - *Bandsawed Block*

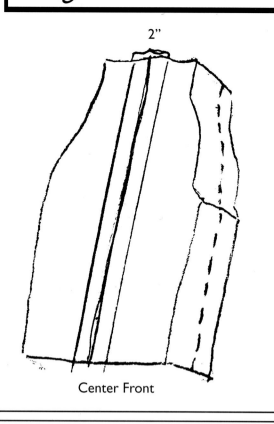

2"

Center Front

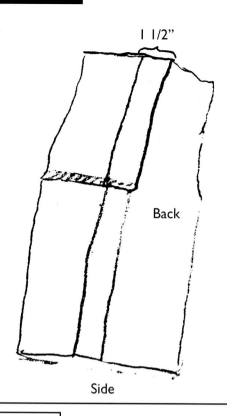

1 1/2"

Back

Side

Diagram A - *Positioning the Nose on the Face*

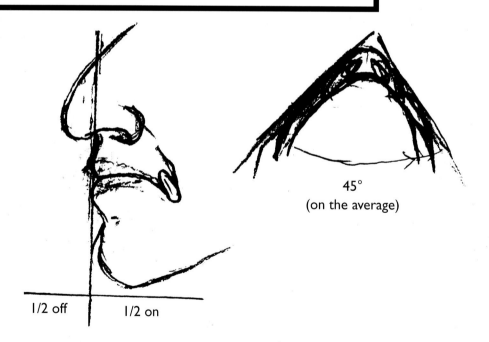

1/2 off   1/2 on

45°
(on the average)

There are some things you should familiarize yourself with when you're ready to carve noses, so let's take a closer look at how the nose fits on the face.

As you'll note in the first part of Diagram A, half of the nose is off the face; half of the nose is on the face. Notice how the nose fits onto the face and how it wraps around the dental curve (which is just another name for the curve of the jaw and the chin). The second part of Diagram A is a view from the chin up. See how the tip of the nose forms a 45 degree angle with the rest of the face?

Diagram B shows several nose profiles. There are, of course, many, many more. For the carving in this book, I'm using the first one on the left.

Diagram C - *Anatomy of the Nose*

 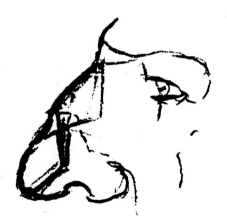

Thinking of the human nose as two overlapping diamonds will help you visualize the shape of the nose. The first diamond starts at the bridge of the nose and extends just past the middle of the nose. The second diamond starts just above the middle of the nose and ends at the tip of the nose. Note that the two diamonds overlap in the center of the nose. These diamonds help you locate the swelled spot where the nasal bone stops and the cartilage starts. It's important to pay attention to the anatomy of the face under the skin. That's what gives a face its structure. This swelled spot, or little flair, doesn't show up in every person as strong as it does in some, but I like to use it because it adds a little bit more to the face. (Taken from "Drawing the Human Head," by Burne Hogarth.)

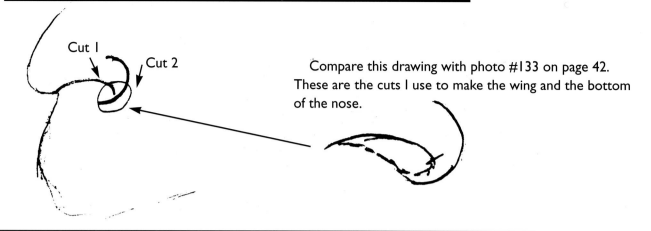

Cut 1

Cut 2

Compare this drawing with photo #133 on page 42. These are the cuts I use to make the wing and the bottom of the nose.

Diagram E - *Mouth Basics*

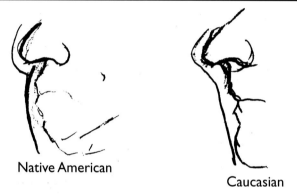

Native American

Caucasian

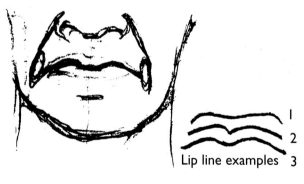

Lip line examples

1
2
3

The five muscles
in the lips

Notice the difference between these two mouth profiles. The drawing on the upper left is the profile of a Native American; the drawing on the upper right is the profile of a Caucasian. There is a pronounced difference in the mouth barrel. I'm carving a mask of a Native American's face in this book, but it's always good to be aware of differences.

In the bottom left drawing, you'll notice that I've divided the mouth area from the bottom of the nose to the chin into three equal parts. The first line is where the actual parting of the lips comes together. The second line is the separation between the bottom lip and the chin (that little horizontal dent we have there). The third line marks the bottom of the chin.

The first line and the third line are pretty much stationary. That horizontal dent (the second line) can move up or down a little bit, depending on the face you're carving. Shifting that will give you a little bit different type of mouth area.

The drawing on the bottom center shows several different examples of lip lines, or the line between two closed lips. These are several that I use frequently, though there are many others.

The five muscles in the lips are shown in the drawing on the bottom right. There are three muscles in the top lip, two muscles in the bottom lip, and one muscle at each corner of the mouth. Look at yourself in the mirror and then smile. You can see the wrinkles. Notice how the mouth won't come all the way to that smile line? There is a little muscle area there in between the smile line and the mouth that creates a kind of stair-step effect.

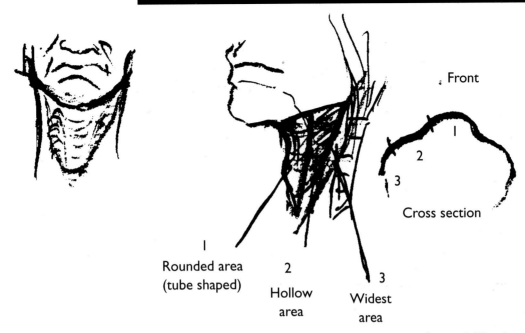

Front

1

2

3

Cross section

1
Rounded area
(tube shaped)

2
Hollow
area

3
Widest
area

This illustration supports photo #167 on page 50. There are three distinct areas to the neck. The first section is the Adam's apple and the little narrow tube that runs right down the center of the neck. The second section is the hollow area that blends off the separation line from the chin and lip. The third section is the widest part of the neck back here under the jaw. You can see these three areas delineated on the front view, the side view and the cross section drawings.

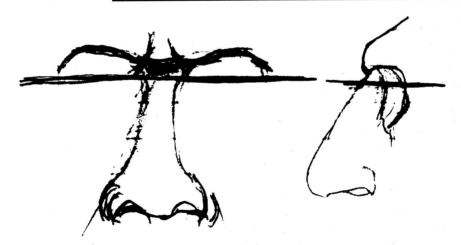

A Native American's head is five eyes wide; a Caucasian's head is four eyes wide. What that basically tells you is that an Indian's eyes might be a little smaller or their heads around their brow area a little wider. You need to be aware of these structural differences when carving faces.

I myself don't measure exactly. The main thing is to allow plenty of space between the eye mounds so that the bridge of the nose doesn't become too narrow. You want to avoid having a little knife-edge nose bridge right there between the eyes.

Notice on the drawing how the centerline of the eye falls a little below the bridge dent of the nose. If you put a pencil right there across the bridge of your nose, you'll notice that you can look right under the pencil. Do this exercise while looking in a mirror. Notice how the center line of the actual eyeball is just below the bridge of the nose.

DIAGRAMS

Diagram H - *Carving the Eye Mound*

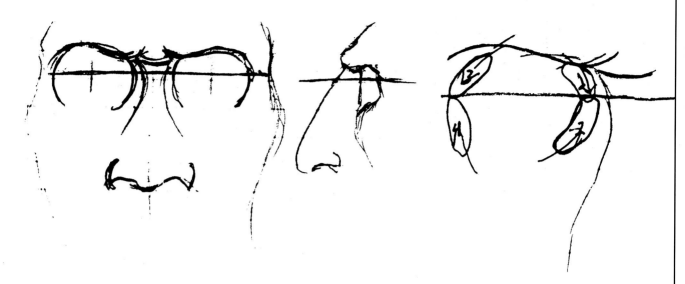

It's important to round the eye mounds from side to side and from the center to the corners. I like to use a little #9 or #7 gouge. These tools work well for creating a nice smooth ball in the eye mound. I want the ball to be round from side to side, straight up and down and a little higher in the center. The diagram shows the positioning of the eye mounds and the directions of the gouge cuts.

Diagram I - *Rounding the Eye Mound*

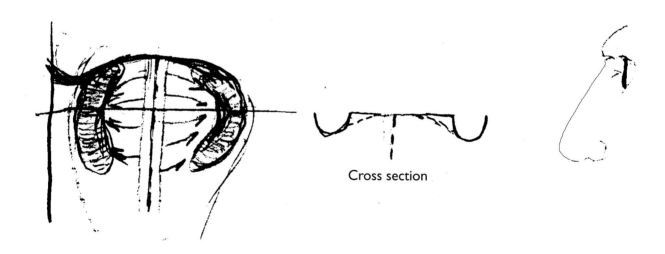

Cross section

Round the eye mound from side to side, not up and down, leaving it higher in the center. You can see the direction of the cuts in the diagram. Notice in the side view drawing how the plane of the eye is straight up and down. The cross section shows more clearly how the eye is rounded from side to side.

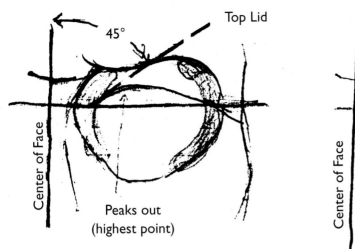

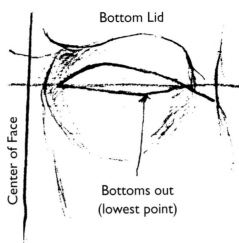

Top Lid

45°

Center of Face

Peaks out
(highest point)

Bottom Lid

Center of Face

Bottoms out
(lowest point)

1. Think "squinty." This will keep you from carving the eyes so they appear too wide open.
2. Don't start too close to the nose.
3. Carry the top lid down past the center on the outside corner.
4. The top lid peaks out before the middle.
5. Bottom lid bottoms out after the middle.
6. The top lid moves; the bottom lid doesn't.

Diagram K - *Cutting the Top Eyelid*

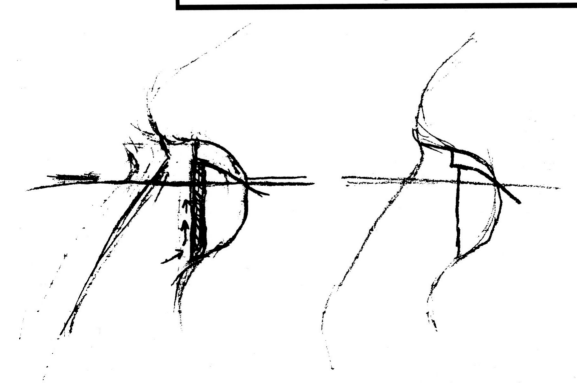

To cut the top eyelid, make a stop cut at the edge of the top eyelid, then shave up to the stop cut. Always start as low as possible on the eye mound. Do not start at the center. Do not cut at an inward angle; cut straight up.

Diagram L - *Cutting the Bottom Eyelid*

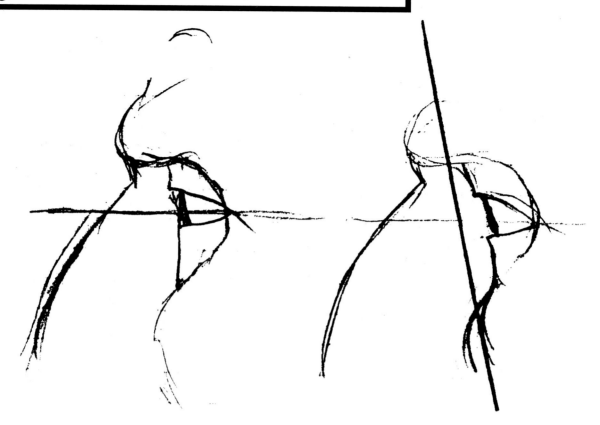

Make a stop cut for the bottom line. Starting at the top lid — not at the centerline — cut or shave the eyeball *down* to the stop cut for the bottom lid. Never cut up toward the top lid.

Notice the angle that the eye sits in the head. See how it tilts in toward the cheek bone and downward? The upper lid sticks out a little farther than the lower lid.

Diagram M - *Wrinkle Pattern*

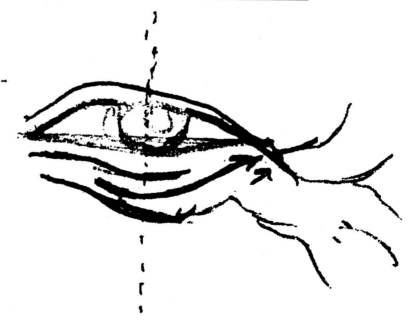

This drawing shows the three basic wrinkle lines under the eye.

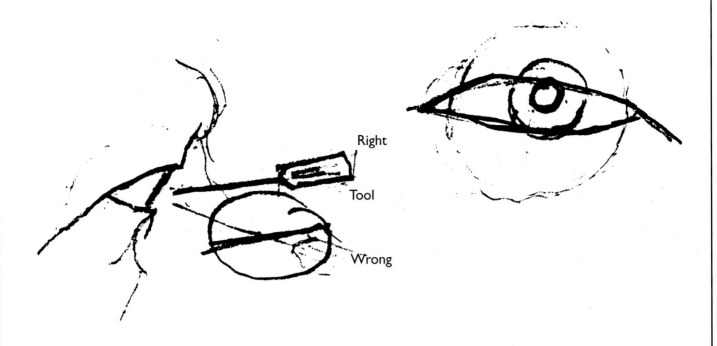

Angle the cut for the pupil slightly downward and out. Don't undercut the pupil. Notice from the drawing how some of the iris (the colored part of the eye) is hidden behind the top eyelid.

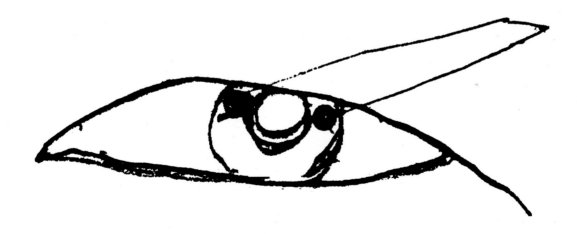

In this carving, the iris (the colored part of the eye) will be removed. Drill two small holes with a regular drill bit to act as pilot holes for the flame burr.

Diagram O - *Wrinkles and Puckers of the Scarf*

Diagram Q - *Carving the Knot*

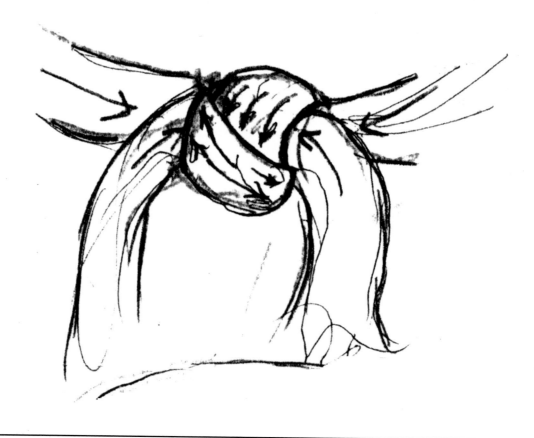

DIAGRAMS

Diagram R -
Profile of a Mask

Pattern

Bandsaw pattern used.
Note: Pattern copied 100% then reduced 50%.

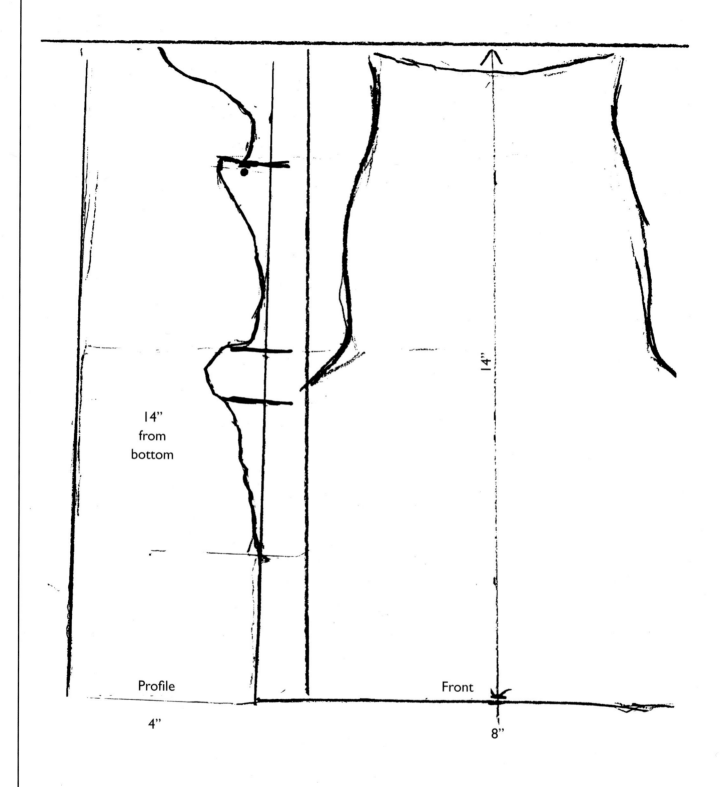

14"
from
bottom

14"

Profile

Front

4"

8"